Ku Hung-Ming

The discourses and sayings of Confucius

A new special translation, illustrated with quotations from Goethe and other

writers

Ku Hung-Ming

The discourses and sayings of Confucius
A new special translation, illustrated with quotations from Goethe and other writers

ISBN/EAN: 9783741101267

Manufactured in Europe, USA, Canada, Australia, Japa

Cover: Foto ©Thomas Meinert / pixelio.de

Manufactured and distributed by brebook publishing software
(www.brebook.com)

Ku Hung-Ming

The discourses and sayings of Confucius

卡立福　存

尼亚大学圖籍館

中國浙江郡長先

時光緒丙午

夏仲

THE

DISCOURSES AND SAYINGS

OF

CONFUCIUS.

論語譯英文

鴻銘先生集譯

松生梁敦彥

茲 在 文 斯

THE
DISCOURSES AND SAYINGS·

OF

CONFUCIUS.

A NEW SPECIAL TRANSLATION, ILLUSTRATED WITH QUOTATIONS
FROM GOETHE AND OTHER WRITERS.

BY

KU HUNG-MING,

M.A., Edin.

Was glänzt, ist fur den Augenblick geboren.
Das Echte, bleibt der Nachwelt unverloren.
GOETHE.

SHANGHAI:
KELLY AND WALSH, LIMITED,
'AND AT
HONGKONG — YOKOHAMA — SINGAPORE.

1898

In Memory

of

A Dead Friend.

T. S. P.

PREFACE.

— ❖ —

IT is now forty years since Dr. LEGGE began the
publication of the first instalment of his translation
of the "Chinese Classics." Any one now, even
without any acquaintance with the Chinese language,
who will take the trouble to turn over the pages of
Dr. LEGGE's translation, cannot help feeling how unsatis-
factory the translation really is. For Dr. LEGGE, from
his raw literary training when he began his work, and
the utter want of critical insight and literary perception
he showed to the end, was really nothing more than a
great sinologue, that is to say, a pundit with a very
learned but dead knowledge of Chinese books. But in
justice to the memory of the great sinologue who, we
regret to hear, has just recently died, it must be said
that notwithstanding the extremely hard and narrow
limits of his mind, which was the result of temperament,
he was, as far as his insight allowed him, thoroughly
conscientious in his work.

To an earnest student who can bring his own
philosophical and literary acumen to study into those
ponderous volumes known as Dr. LEGGE's translation
of the "Chinese Classics," no doubt some insight into

the moral culture, or what is called the civilisation of the Chinese people, will reveal itself. But to the generality of the English reading people we cannot but think the intellectual and moral outfit of the Chinaman as presented by Dr. LEGGE in his translation of the Chinese books, must appear as strange and grotesque as to an ordinary Englishman's eyes, unaccustomed to it, the Chinaman's costume and outward appearance.

The attempt is therefore here made to render this little book, which, of all books written in the Chinese language, we believe, is *the* book which gives to the Chinaman his intellectual and moral outfit, accessible to the general English reader. With this object in view, we have tried to make Confucius and his disciples speak in the same way as an educated Englishman would speak had he to express the same thoughts which the Chinese worthies had to express. In order further to take away as much as possible the sense of strangeness and peculiarity for the English readers, we have, whenever it is possible to do so, eliminated all Chinese proper names. Lastly, with the hope of bringing home, so to speak, the significance of the thought in the text, we have added as notes quotations from well known European authors, which, by calling up the train of thought already familiar, may perhaps appeal to readers acquainted with those authors.

We take the opportunity here of paying our
tribute of respect to the memory of an Englishman,
Sir CHALONER ALABASTER, who has at different periods
published masterful translations of many portions of
this book. When in Canton ten years ago, we urged
upon him to seriously undertake the translation of the
Chinese sacred books, with Dr. LEGGE's translations
of which we were both dissatisfied. But he was very
conscientious. He said that his knowledge of Chinese
books and literature was too limited; besides, that he
was not a "literary man." He in turn advised us to
undertake the work. Now, after ten years, just as
we finish this first attempt to follow his advice, the
melancholy news comes that he, to whom our little
work would have been of some interest, has passed
away from among living men.

We have said that this little book, which contains
the digested sayings and discourses of Confucius and
his disciples—presenting in a very small compass what
the late Mr. MATTHEW ARNOLD would call a "criticism
of life,"—is the book which gives to the Chinaman his
intellectual and moral outfit. Of the nature and value
of that outfit we do not feel ourselves called upon here
to express an opinion. We will only here express
the hope that educated and thinking Englishmen who

will take the trouble to read this translation of ours, may, after reading it, be led to reconsider their hitherto foregone conceptions of the Chinese people, and in so doing be enabled not only to modify their preconceptions of the Chinese people, but also to change the attitude of their personal and national relations with the Chinese as individuals and as a nation.

KU HUNG-MING.

Viceroy's Yamen,
  Wuchang,
    1st August 1898.

INDEX TO CHAPTERS.

THE
DISCOURSES AND SAYINGS
OF
CONFUCIUS.

CHAPTER I.

1. Confucius remarked, "It is indeed a pleasure to acquire knowledge and, as you go on acquiring, to put into practice what you have acquired. A greater pleasure still it is when friends of congenial minds come from afar to seek you because of your attainments. But he is truly a wise and good man who feels no discomposure even when he is not noticed of men."

2. A disciple of Confucius remarked, "A man who is a good son and a good citizen will seldom be found to be a man disposed to quarrel with those in authority over him ; and men who are not disposed to quarrel with those in authority will never be found to disturb the peace and order of the State.

"A wise man devotes his attention to what is essential in the foundation of life. When the founda-

2

tion is laid, wisdom will come.   Now, to be a good son and a good citizen—do not these form the foundation of a moral life ? "

3. Confucius remarked, " With plausible speech and fine manners will seldom be found moral character."

4. A disciple of Confucius remarked, " I daily examine into my personal conduct on three points :— First, whether in carrying out the duties entrusted to me by others, I have not failed in conscientiousness ; Secondly, whether in intercourse with friends, I have not failed in sincerity and trustworthiness ; Thirdly, whether I have not failed to practice what I profess in my teaching."

5. Confucius remarked, " When directing the affairs of a great nation, a man must be serious in attention to business and faithful and punctual in his engagements. He must study economy in the public expenditure, and love the welfare of the people.   He must employ the people at the proper time of the year."[1]

6. Confucius remarked, " A young man, when at home, should be a good son ; when out in the world, a good citizen.   He should be circumspect and truthful. He should be in sympathy with all men, but intimate

[1] In ancient China the people were lightly taxed, but were liable to forced labour and conscription in times of war.

with men of moral character. If he has time and
opportunity to spare, after the performance of those
duties, he should then employ them in literary pursuits."

7. A disciple of Confucius remarked, "A man who
can love worthiness in man as he loves beauty in
woman; who in his duties to his parents is ready to do
his utmost, and in the service of his prince is ready to
give up his life; who in intercourse with friends is found
trustworthy in what he says,—such a man, although
men may say of him that he is an uneducated man, I
must consider him to be really an educated man."

8. Confucius remarked, "A wise man who is not
serious will not inspire respect; what he learns will
not remain permanent.

"Make conscientiousness and sincerity your first
principles.

"Have no friends who are not as yourself.

"When you have bad habits do not hesitate to
change them."

9. A disciple of Confucius remarked, "By
cultivating respect for the dead, and carrying the
memory back to the distant past[2], the moral feeling of
the people will waken and grow in depth."

---

[2] Cogitavi dies antiquos et annos æternos in mente habui.—*Psalm* lxxvii, 5.

10. A man once asked a disciple of Confucius, saying, "How was it that whenever the Master came into a country he was always informed of the actual state and policy of its government? Did he seek for the information or was it given to him?"

"The Master," replied the disciple, "was gracious, simple, earnest, modest and courteous; therefore he could obtain what information he wanted. The Master's way of obtaining information—well, it was different from other people's ways."

11. Confucius remarked, "When a man's father is living the son should have regard to what his father would have him do; when the father is dead, to what his father has done. A son who for three years after his father's death does not in his own life change his father's principles, may be said to be a good son."

12. A disciple of Confucius remarked, "In the practice of art,' what is valuable is natural spontaneity.

* Dr. LEGGE says of the Chinese word 禮, which we have here translated "art," that it is a word not easily rendered in another language. On the other hand, Mr. B. H. CHAMBERLAIN, in his book *Things Japanese*, remarks that the Japanese language [China and Japan have the same written language] has no genuine native word for "art."

The English word "art," if we mistake not, is used in various senses to express: 1st, a work of art; 2nd, the practice of art; 3rd, artificial as opposed to natural; 4th, the principle of art as opposed to the principle of nature; 5th, the strict principle of art. In this last sense of the use of the English word "art" lies, as Dr. LEGGE says of the Chinese word mentioned above, "the idea of what is proper" and fit, τὸ πρέπον, in all *relations* of things.

According to the rules of art held by the ancient kings it was this quality in a work of art which constituted its excellence ; in great as well as in small things they were guided by this principle.

"But in being natural there is something not permitted. To know that it is necessary to be natural without restraining the impulse to be natural by the strict principle of art,—that is something not permitted."

13. A disciple of Confucius remarked, "If you make promises within the bounds of what is right, you will be able to keep your word. If you confine earnestness within the bounds of judgment and good taste, you will keep out of discomfiture and insult. If you make friends of those with whom you ought to, you will be able to depend upon them."

For those who may be interested in the subject, we may here mention that the modern Japanese invention, *bi-jutsu* 美術 (beautiful legerdemain) for "art" is not a happy one. The proper term in Chinese for a work of art would be 文物 ; for the practice of art, 藝. In fact, the Japanese word *Geisha* 藝師 means literally an *artiste*. As for the use of the term "art" in the sense of "artificial" as opposed to something "natural," the philosopher Chuang Ts uses 人 (human) and 天 (divine).

Then "the principle of art, not taken by itself, but as opposed to the principle of nature, would be in Chinese 文 for "art" and 質 for "nature." Such a sentence as that of GOETHE, for instance, "Art is called Art, because it is not Nature," would be rendered into Chinese or Japanese thus : 文之所以謂 之文爲其非質也. Chinese art critics also speak of 化工 creative art and 藝工 imitative art. Finally, we may as well add, the Chinese term for mechanical art or the practice of it is 技術.

14. Confucius remarked, "A wise and good man, in matters of food, should never seek to indulge his appetite; in lodging, he should not be too solicitous of comfort. He should be diligent in business and careful in speech. He should seek for the company of men of virtue and learning, in order to profit by their lessons and example. In this way he may become a man of real culture."

15. A disciple of Confucius said to him, "To be poor and yet not to be servile; to be rich and yet not to be proud, what do you say to that?"

"It is good," replied Confucius, "but better still it is to be poor and yet contented; to be rich and yet know how to be courteous."

"I understand," answered the disciple :

> 'We must cut, we must file,
> 'Must chisel and must grind.'

That is what you mean, is it not?"

"My friend," replied Confucius, "now I can begin to speak of poetry to you. I see you understand how to apply the moral."

16. Confucius remarked, "One should not be concerned not to be understood of men; one should be concerned not to understand men."

CHAPTER II.

1. Confucius remarked, " He who rules the people, depending upon the moral sentiment, is like the Pole-star, which keeps its place while all the other stars revolve round it."

2. Confucius remarked, " The Book of Ballads, Songs and Psalms[4] contains three hundred pieces. The moral of them all may be summed up in one sentence : ' Have no evil thoughts.' "

3. Confucius remarked, "If in government you depend upon laws, and maintain order by enforcing those laws by punishments, you can also make the people keep away from wrong-doing, but they will lose the sense of shame for wrong-doing. If, on the other hand, in government you depend upon the moral sentiment, and maintain order by encouraging education and good manners, the people will have a sense of shame for wrong-doing and, moreover, will emulate what is good."

4. Confucius remarked, " At fifteen I had made up my mind to give myself up to serious studies.   At

[4] Now called the Canon of Poetry, one of the so-called five Classics, in the Bible of China.

thirty I had formed my opinions and judgment. At forty
I had no more doubts. At fifty I understood the truth
in religion. At sixty I could understand whatever I heard
without exertion. At seventy I could follow whatever
my heart desired without transgressing the law."

5. A noble of the Court in Confucius' native
State asked him what constituted the duty of a good
son. Confucius answered, "Do not fail in what is
required of you."

Afterwards, as a disciple was driving him in his
carriage, Confucius told the disciple, saying, "My Lord
M—— asked me what constituted the duty of a good
son, and I answered, 'Do not fail in what is required of
you.'"

"What did you mean by that?" asked the disciple.

"I meant," replied Confucius, "when his parents
are living, a good son should do his duties to them
according to the usage prescribed by propriety ; when
they are dead, he should bury them and honour their
memory according to the rites prescribed by propriety."

6. A son of the noble mentioned above put the
same question to Confucius as his father did. Confucius
answered, "Think how anxious your parents are when
you are sick, and you will know your duty towards
them."

7. A disciple of Confucius asked him the same question as the above. Confucius answered, "The duty of a good son nowadays means only to be able to support his parents. But you also keep your dogs and horses alive. If there is no feeling of love and respect, where is the difference?"

9. Another disciple asked the same question. Confucius answered, "The difficulty is with the expression of your look. That merely when anything is to be done the young people do it, and when there is food and wine the old folk are allowed to enjoy it,—do you think that is the whole duty of a good son?"

10. Confucius, speaking of a favourite disciple whose name was Yen Hui,* remarked, "I have talked with him for one whole day, during which he has never once raised one single objection to what I have said, as if he were dull of understanding. But when he has retired, on examining into his life and conversation I find he has been able to profit by what I have said to him. No—he is not a man dull of understanding."

* The St. John of the Confucian gospel,—a pure, heroic, ideal character, the disciple whom the Master loved. As the name of this disciple occurs very frequently thoughout the book, we here depart from our rule of eliminating all Chinese proper names, and shall hereafter always introduce him by name.

10. Confucius remarked, "You look at how a man acts; consider his motives; find out his tastes. How can a man hide himself; how can he hide himself from you?"

11. Confucius remarked, "If a man will constantly go over what he has acquired and keep continually adding to it new acquirements, he may become a teacher of men."

12. Confucius remarked, "A wise man will not make himself into a mere machine fit only to do one kind of work."

13. A disciple enquired what constituted a wise and good man. Confucius answered, "A wise and good man is one who acts before he speaks, and afterwards speaks according to his actions."

14. Confucius remarked, "A wise man is impartial, not neutral. A fool is neutral but not impartial."

15. Confucius remarked, "Study without thinking is labour lost. Thinking without study is perilous."

16. Confucius remarked, "To give oneself up to the study of metaphysical theories—that is very injurious indeed."

17. Confucius said to a disciple, "Shall I teach you what is understanding? To know what it is that you know, and to know what it is that you do not know,—that is understanding."

18. A disciple was studying with a view to preferment. Confucius said to him, "Read and learn everything, but suspend your judgment on anything of which
you are in doubt ; for the rest, be careful in what you
say : in that way you will give few occasions for men
to criticise what you say. Mix with the world and see
everything, but keep away and do not meddle with
anything which may bring you into trouble ; for the
rest, be careful in what you do : in that way you will
have few occasions for self-reproach.

"Now if in your conversation you give few
occasions for men to criticise you, and in your conduct
you have few occasions for self-reproach, you cannot
help getting preferment, even if you would."

19. The reigning prince of his native State asked
Confucius what should be done to secure the submis-
sion of the people. Confucius answered, "Uphold
the cause of the just and put down every cause that
is unjust, and the people will submit. But uphold the
cause of the unjust and put down every cause that is
just, then the people will not submit."

20. A noble who was the minister in power in the
government in Confucius' native State asked him what
should be done to inspire a feeling of respect and
loyalty in the people, in order to make them exert

themselves for the good of the country. Confucius answered, "Treat them with seriousness and they will respect you. Let them see that you honour your parents and your prince, and are considerate for the welfare of those under you, and the people will be loyal to you. Advance those who excel in anything and educate the ignorant, and the people will exert themselves."

21. Somebody asked Confucius, saying, "Why are you not taking part in the government of the country?"

Confucius answered, "What does the 'Book of Records' say of the duties of a good son?

"'Be dutiful to your parents; be brotherly to your brothers; discharge your duties in the government of your family.' These, then, are also duties of government. Why then must one take part in the government of the country in order to discharge the duties of government?"

22. Confucius remarked, "I do not know how men get along without good faith. A cart without a yoke and a carriage without harness,—how could they go?"

23. A disciple asked Confucius whether ten generations after their time the state of the civilisation of the world⁺ could be known.

* *i.e.* China.

Confucius answered, "The House of Yin adopted the civilisation of the Hsia dynasty; what modifications they made is known. The present Chou dynasty adopted the civilisation of the House of Yin; what modifications this last dynasty made are also known. Perhaps some other may hereafter take the place of the present Chou dynasty; but should that happen a hundred generations after this, the state of the civilisation of the world [7] then, can be known."

24. Confucius remarked, "To worship a spirit to whom one is not bound by a real feeling of duty or respect is idolatry[8]; to see what is right and to act against one's judgment shows a want of courage."

---

[7] *i.e.* China. The period of the Hsia dynasty [B.C. 2205-1818] was to a man in China of Confucius' time what the period of the Greek history would be to a modern man of Europe to-day. The Yin dynasty [B.C. 1766-1154] was, in like manner, what the period of the Roman history would be to a modern man.

[8] Literally "servility." "C'est une malheur des gens honnêtes qu'ils sont des lâches."—*Voltaire.* (It is a misfortune of good people that they are dastards.)

CHAPTER   III.

1. The head of a powerful family of nobles in
Confucius' native State employed eight sets of choristers
[an Imperial prerogative] in their family chapel.
Confucius, remarking on this, was heard to say, "If
this is allowed to pass, what may not be allowed ?"

2. The members of the same powerful family
mentioned above concluded the service in their chapel
by chanting the hymn used only on occasions of
Imperial worship.   Confucius remarked on it, saying :
"The words of the hymn begin—

> ' Surrounded by his nobles and princes,
> ' August the Son of Heaven looks ; '

"Now what is there in the chapel of this noble family
to which those words of the hymn can be applied ?"

3. Confucius remarked, "If a man is without moral
character, what good can the use of the fine arts do
him ?   If a man is without moral character, what good
can the use of music do him ?"

4. A disciple asked what constituted the funda-
mental principle of art.

"That is a very great question," replied Confucius, "but in the art used in social usages it is better to be simple than to be expensive ; in rituals for the dead, it is better that there should be heartfelt grief than minute attention to observances."

5. Confucius remarked, "The heathen hordes of the North and East, even, acknowledge the authority of their chiefs, whereas now in China respect for authority no longer exists anywhere." *

6. The head of the powerful family of nobles mentioned in section 1 of this chapter was going to offer sacrifice on the top of the Great T'ai Mountain [an Imperial prerogative]. Confucius then said to a disciple who was in the service of the noble, "Can you not do anything to save him from this ?" "No," replied the disciple, "I cannot." "Ah, then," answered Confucius, "it is useless to say anything more. But, really, do you think that the Spirit of the Great Mountain is not as Lin-fang ?" [10]

---

* The watchword of Chinese chivalry is 尊 王 攘 夷 (Honour the king and break the heathen). These four words, taken in their true sense and not in their common vulgar sense, have created the modern Japan of to-day.

TENNYSON, interpreting the chivalry of Europe in the dialect of Europe, makes his knights of chivalry swear :—" To reverence the king as if he were their conscience, and their conscience as their king. To break the heathen and uphold the Christ."

[10] The name of the disciple who asked the question in section 4 of this chapter. The point in the reference in this last sentence, we confess, we do not understand.

7. Confucius remarked, "A gentleman never *competes* in anything he does,—except perhaps in archery. But even then, when he wins he courteously makes his bow before he advances to take his place among the winners ; and, when he has lost he walks down and drinks his cup of forfeit. Thus, even in this case of competition, he shows himself to be a gentleman."

8. A disciple asked Confucius for the meaning of the following verse :

> Her coquettish smiles,
>   How dimpling they are ;
> Her beautiful eyes,
>   How beaming they are ;
> O fairest is she
>   Who is simple and plain.

"In painting," answered Confucius, "ornamentation and colour are matters of secondary importance compared with the groundwork."

"Then art itself," said the disciple, "is a matter of "secondary consideration ?"

"My friend," replied Confucius, "You have given me an idea. Now I can talk of poetry with you." [11]

[11] Beauty unadorned is adorned the most ; the last line in Chinese is an exact translation of Horace's "simplex munditiis." The English student may here remember Tom Moore's lines :—

> "Lesbia has a beaming eye,
> But no one knows on whom it beameth."

9. Confucius remarked to a disciple, "I can tell you of the state of the arts and civilisation during the Hsia dynasty [say the Greek civilisation];[12] but the modern State of Ts'i [say modern Greece] cannot furnish sufficient evidence to prove what I say. I can tell you of the state of the arts and civilisation during the Yin dynasty [say Roman civilisation]; but the modern state of Sung [say Italy] cannot furnish sufficient evidence to prove what I say. The reason is because the literary monuments extant are too meagre,—otherwise I could prove to you what I say."

10. Confucius remarked, "At the service of the great Ti sacrifice [the 'Mass' in ancient China], I always make it a point to leave as soon as the pouring of the libation on the ground is over."

11. Somebody asked Confucius for the meaning of the great Ti sacrifice mentioned above.

"I do not know," answered Confucius. "One who understands its significance will find it as easy to rule the world as to look at this—thus:" pointing to the palm of his hand.

12. Confucius worshipped the dead as if he actually felt the presence of the departed ones. He

[12] *See* Note, Chapter II, Section 23.

4

worshipped the Spiritual Powers as if he actually felt the presence of the Powers.

He once remarked, "If I cannot give up heart and soul when I am worshipping, I always consider as if I have not worshipped."

13. An officer in a certain State asked Confucius, saying, "What is meant by the common saying 'It is better to pray to the God of the Hearth than to the God of the House?'"

"Not so," replied Confucius, "a man who has sinned against God,—it is useless for him to pray anywhere at all."

14. Confucius remarked, "The civilisation of the present Chou dynasty is founded on the civilisations of the two preceding dynasties. How splendidly rich it is in all the arts! I prefer the present Chou civilisation."

15. When Confucius first attended the service at the State Cathedral (Ancestral Temple of the reigning prince), he enquired as to what he should do at every stage of the service. Somebody thereupon remarked, "Who tells me that the son of the plebeian of Ts'ow [13] is a man who knows the correct forms?"

[13] A district where Confucius' father had been Chief Magistrate.

When Confucius heard of the remark, he said, " *That* is the correct form."

16. Confucius remarked, "In archery, putting the arrow *through* the target should not count as points, because the competitors cannot all be expected to be equal in mere physical strength. At least, that was the old rule."

17. A disciple wanted to dispense with the sheep offered in sacrifice in the religious ceremony held at the beginning of every month.

" What *you* would save," said Confucius to him, " is the cost of the sheep ; what *I* would save is the principle of the rite."

18. Confucius remarked, " Men now account it servile to pay to their prince all the honours due to him."[14]

19. The reigning prince of Confucius' native State asked Confucius how a prince should treat his public servant and how a public servant should behave to his prince.

"Let the prince," answered Confucius, "treat his public servant with honour. The public servant must serve the prince, his master, with loyalty."

[14] *See* Note, Section 5 of this Chapter.

20. Confucius remarked, "The first ballad in the Book of Ballads and Songs[15] expresses the emotions of love. It is passionate, but not sensual; it is melancholy, but not morbid."

21. The reigning prince of Confucius' native State asked a disciple of Confucius about the emblems used on the altars to the Titular Genius of the land.[16]

The disciple answered, "The sovereigns of the House of Hsia planted the pine tree;[16] the people of the Yin dynasty adopted the cypress; and the people of the present Chou dynasty has chosen the *li* (chestnut) tree as a symbol of awe (*li*) to the population."

When Confucius afterwards heard of what the disciple said, he remarked, "It is useless to speak of a thing that is done; to change a course that is begun; or to blame what is past and gone."

22. Confucius, speaking of a famous statesman (the Bismarck of the time), remarked, "Kuan Chung was by no means a great-minded man!"

"But," said somebody, "Kuan Chung was simple in his life: was he not?"

[15] *See* Note, Chapter II, Section 2.
[16] The adoption of these emblems in old China is like the modern emblems of the "Rose" for England and of "Fleur de lys" for the House of Bourbon in France.

"Why," replied Confucius, " Kuan Chung had that magnificent Sansouci Pleasaunce of his. Besides, he had a special officer appointed to every function in his household. How can one say that he was simple in his life ? "

"Well," rejoined the enquirer, "but still, Kuan Chung was a man of taste who observed the correct forms ; was he not ? "

" No," answered Confucius, " The reigning princes have walls built before their palace gates. Kuan Chung also had a wall built before his door. When two reigning princes meet, each has a special *buffet*. Kuan Chung also had his special buffet. If you say Kuan Chung was a man of taste, who is not a man of taste ? " [17]

23. Confucius remarked to the Grand Kapel Meister of his native State, " I think I know the way in which a piece should be played with a full orchestra. At first, the full volume of sound in the piece should be heard. Then, as you proceed, you must pay attention to and bring out each note of the piece, distinct and clear, but flowing, as it were, without break or interval,—thus to the end."

[17] It is curious that Kuan Chung, the Bismarck of ancient China, adopted the same motto in politics as that famous motto of the modern Founder of the German Empire—*Do, ut des*—in Chinese 欲取之故與之.

24. An officer in command of a certain Pass on the frontier where Confucius on his travels was passing, asked for the permission to be presented to him ; saying, "Whenever a wise man passes this way, I have always had the honour to wait upon him." Confucius' disciples accordingly presented him.

When the officer came out of the interview he said to the disciples, "Gentlemen, why should you be concerned at your present want of official position ! The world has long been without the order and justice of good government ; now God is going to make use of your Teacher as a tocsin to awaken the world."

25. Confucius, speaking of a famous piece of music (the most ancient then known in China), remarked, " It has all the excellence of the physical beauty of harmony ; it has also all the excellence of moral grandeur." Speaking of another piece, of a more recent date, Confucius remarked, "It has all the excellence of the physical beauty of harmony ; but it has not all the excellence of moral grandeur."

26. Confucius remarked, "Possession of power without generosity ; courtesy without seriousness ; mourning without grief,—I have no desire to look at such a state of things."

CHAPTER IV.

1. Confucius remarked, "It is the moral life of a neighbourhood which constitutes its excellence. He is not an intelligent man, who, in choosing his residence, does not select a place with a moral surrounding."

2. Confucius remarked, "A man without moral character cannot long put up with adversity, nor can he long enjoy prosperity.

"Men of moral character find themselves at home in being moral ; men of intelligence find it advantageous to be moral."

3. Confucius remarked, "It is only men of moral character who know how to love men or to hate men."

4. Confucius remarked, "If you fix your mind upon a moral life, you will be free from evil."

5. Confucius remarked, "Riches and honours are objects of men's desire ; but if I cannot have them without leaving the path of duty, 1 would not have them. Poverty and a low position in life are objects of men's dislike ; but if I cannot leave them without departing from the path of duty, I would not leave them.

"A wise man who leaves his moral character is no longer entitled to the name of a wise man. A wise man never for one single moment in his life loses sight of a moral life; in moments of haste and hurry, as in moments of danger and peril, he always clings to it."

6. Confucius remarked, "I do not now see a man who really loves a moral life ; or one who really hates an immoral life. One who really loves a moral life would esteem nothing above it. One who really hates an immoral life would be a moral man who would not allow anything the least immoral in his life.

"Nevertheless, if a man were really to exert himself for one single day to live a moral life, I do not believe he will find that he has not the strength to do it. At least I have never heard of such a case."

7. Confucius remarked, "Men's faults are characteristic. By observing a man's failings you can judge of his moral character."

8. Confucius remarked, "When a man has learnt wisdom in the morning, he may be content to die in the evening before the sun sets."

9. Confucius remarked, "It is useless to speak to a gentleman who wants to give himself up to serious studies and who yet is ashamed because of his poor food or bad clothes."

10. Confucius remarked, "A wise man in his judgment of the world, has no predilections nor prejudices ; he is on the side of what is right."

11. Confucius remarked, " A wise man regards the moral worth of a man ; a fool, only his position.[18] A wise man expects justice ; a fool expects favours."

12. Confucius remarked, " If you always look only to your own advantage you will be sure to make many enemies."

13. Confucius remarked, "He who can rule a country by real courtesy and good manners that are in him, will find no difficulty in doing it. But a ruler who has no real courtesy and good manners in him, what can the mere rules of etiquette and formality avail him."

14. Confucius remarked, "Be not concerned for want of a position ; be concerned how to fit yourself for a position. Be not concerned that you are not known, but seek to do something to deserve a reputation."

15. Confucius remarked to a disciple, "In all my life and teaching there is one underlying

[18] We venture to think that there is a palpable misprint here in the text of 土, " earth," for " position " 位, which has hitherto escaped all Chinese commentators. The old seal characters for the two words are identical ; hence the misprint.

5

connected principle." "Even so," answered the disciple.

Afterwards, when Confucius had left, the other disciples asked the disciple who was above spoken to, "What did the master mean by what he said just now?" "The principle in the master's life and teaching," answered the disciple, "is comprised in the two words: conscientiousness and charity."

16. Confucius remarked, "A wise man sees what is right in a question; a fool, what is advantageous to himself."[19]

17. Confucius remarked, "When we meet with men of worth, we should think how we may equal them. When we meet with worthless men, we should turn into ourselves and find out if we do not resemble them."

18. Confucius remarked, "In serving his parents a son should seldom remonstrate with them; but if he was obliged to do so, and should find that they will not listen, he should yet not fail in respect nor disregard their wishes; however much trouble they may give him, he should never complain."

[19] Sir CHALONER ALABASTER translates thus: "The gentleman regards what is right; the cad regards what will pay."

19. Confucius remarked, "While his parents are living, a son should not go far abroad; if he does, he should let them know where he goes."

20. Confucius remarked, "A son who for three years after his father's death does not, in his own life, change his father's principles, may be considered to be a good son."

21. Confucius remarked, "A son should always keep in mind the age of his parents, as a matter for thankfulness as well as for anxiety."

22. Confucius remarked, "Men of old kept silence for fear lest what they said should not come up to what they did."

23. Confucius remarked, "He who wants little[20] seldom goes wrong."

24. Confucius remarked, "A wise man wants to be slow in speech and diligent in conduct."

25. Confucius remarked, "Moral worth is never left alone; society is sure to grow round him."

26. A disciple of Confucius remarked, "In the service of your prince, if you keep constantly pointing out his errors it will lead to your disgrace; if you act in the same way to your friends it will estrange them."

[20] Better, perhaps, "He who confines his sphere."

"You will find, on the average, fewer bad economists in the country than in the towns; fewer again in small towns than in large ones. Why? Man is intended for a limited condition."—*Goethe.*

CHAPTER V.

1. Confucius remarked of a disciple, saying, "No man need hesitate to give his daughter to such a man to wife. It is true he has been in prison, but it was through no crime of his."

Confucius accordingly gave him his own daughter to wife.

Confucius remarked of another disciple, saying, "When there is order and justice in the government of the country, he will not be neglected. But should there be no order and justice in the government of the country, he will escape persecution."

Confucius accordingly gave his niece to him to wife.

2. Confucius then went on to remark of another disciple saying, "What a wise and good man he is! I wonder if there were no wise and good men in the country, how that man could have acquired the character he has."

3. Another disciple who heard the above remarks said then to Confucius, "And I, what do you say of

me?"   "You are," answered Confucius, "a work of art."   "What work of art?" asked the other.   "A rich jewelled work of art," was the reply.

4. Somebody remarked of a disciple of Confucius, saying, " He is a good moral man, but he is not a man of ready wit."

When Confucius heard the remark, he said, " What is the good of a ready wit? A man who is always ready with his tongue to others will only often make enemies. I do not know if he is a moral man, but I do not see the good of having a ready wit."

5. Confucius on one occasion wanted a disciple to enter public life.   " No," answered the disciple, " I have not yet confidence in myself."   Thereupon Confucius commended him.

6. Confucius on one occasion remarked, " There is no order and justice now in the government in China. I will betake me to a ship and sail over the sea to seek for it in other countries.   If I take anybody with me, I will take Yu,"[21] referring to a disciple.

The disciple referred to, when he heard of what Confucius said, was glad, and offered to go.

[21] The St. Peter of the Confucian gospel ; a brave, intrepid, impetuous, chivalrous character.   His name is Chung Yu, Chi-lu being his honorific name.   We make exception to our rule in his case, as in the case of Yen Hui, mentioned in Chapter II, Section 9.

"My friend," said Confucius then to him, "You have certainly more courage than I have; only you do not exercise judgment when using it."

7. A member of a powerful family of nobles in Confucius' native State asked Confucius if his disciple, the above mentioned Chung Yu, was a moral character. "I cannot say," answered Confucius. But on being pressed, Confucius said, "In the government of a State of even the first-rate power the man could be entrusted with the organisation of the army. I cannot say if he could be called a moral character."

The noble then put the same question with regard to another disciple. Confucius answered, " In the government of a large town or in the direction of affairs in a small principality, the man could be entrusted with the chief authority. I cannot say if he could be called a moral character."

The noble went on to put the same question with regard to another disciple. Confucius answered, "At court, in a gala-dress reception, he could be entrusted with the duty of entertaining the visitors. I cannot say if he could be called a moral character."

8. Confucius once said to a disciple, "You and Hui (the favourite Yen Hui), who is the abler man?"

The disciple answered, " How should I dare compare myself with him. When he has learnt one thing he immediately understands its application to all cases ; whereas I, when I have learnt one thing I can only follow out its bearing and applications to one or two particular cases."

9. A disciple of Confucius spent the best hours of the day in sleep. Confucius, remarking on it, said : "You cannot carve anything out of rotten wood nor plaster up a wall built up of rubbish. What is the use of rebuke in such a case ?"

Confucius then went on to say, " At one time, when I wanted to judge of a man, I listened to what he said, and I knew for certain what he would do in his life. But now, when I want to judge of a man, I have to look at what he does in his life as well as listen to what he says. It is, perhaps, men like this young man who have made me change my method of judging men."

10. Confucius once remarked, " I do not now see a man of strong character." " There is So-and-so," said somebody. " No," replied Confucius, " he is a man of strong passions ; he is not a man of strong character."

11. A disciple said to Confucius, " What I do not wish that others should (not) do unto me, I also do not wish that I should do unto them." " My friend,"

answered Confucius, "You have not yet attained to that."

12. A disciple of Confucius remarked, "You will often hear the master speak on the subjects of art and literature, but you will never hear him speak on the subjects of metaphysics or theology."

13. When Confucius' disciple, the intrepid Chung Yu, had learnt anything which he was not yet able to carry out into practice, he was afraid to learn anything new.

14. A disciple, speaking of an ancient worthy of the time, enquired of Confucius saying, "How was it that he had the title of 'Beau-clerc' added as an honour to his name after his death?"

"He was," answered Confucius, "a man of great industry, who applied himself to self-culture; he was not ashamed to seek for information from others more ignorant than himself. For that reason he has had the title of "Beau-clerc" added as a honour to his name after his death."

15. Confucius remarked of a famous statesman (the Colbert of the time), saying, "He showed himself to be a good and wise man in four ways. In his conduct of himself he was earnest, and in serving the interests of his prince he was serious. In providing for the wants

of the people, he was generous, and in dealing with them he was just."

16. Confucius remarked of another famous states-man (the Sir William Temple of the time), saying : " He knew how to observe the true relations in friend-ship. However long-standing his acquaintance with a man might be, he always maintained throughout the same invariable careful respect."

17. Confucius remarked of an eccentric character of the time, saying, " The man actually built a chapel elaborate with carvings for a large tortoise which he kept. What can one say of the intellect of a man like that ? "

18. A disciple of Confucius asked him to give his opinion of a public character of the time, saying, " In his public life three times he was made Prime Minister, and yet on none of these occasions did he show the least signs of elation. Three times he was dismissed from office, and also on none of these occasions did he show the least signs of disappointment. He was care-ful every time, when giving up office, to explain to his successor the line of policy which the Government under him hitherto had been pursuing."

" Now," asked the disciple, " what do you think of him ?"

6

"He was," answered Confucius, "a conscientious man." "But," asked the disciple, "could he be called a moral character?" "I cannot say," replied Confucius, "if he could be called a moral character."

The disciple then went on to ask about another public character, saying, "When the Prime Minister in his native State murdered the prince, his master, that worthy had large possessions in the country, but he threw them all away and quitted the country. Arriving at another State, he remarked, 'I see here they are all parricides, the same as our parricide minister at home;" and immediately again quitted that country. Thus he went on from one State to another, making the same observation. Now, what do you think of this man?"

"He was," replied Confucius, "a pure, high-minded man." "But," asked the disciple, "could he be called a moral character?" "I cannot say," answered Confucius, "if he could be called a moral character."

19. It was remarked of a public character of the time that he always reflected thrice over every time before he.acted. When Confucius heard of the remark, he observed, "Think *twice*—that is sufficient."

20. Confucius remarked of a public character of the time, saying, "He was a man who, when there was order and justice in the government of the country,

acted as a man of great understanding. But when there was no order and justice in the government of the country, he acted as if he was a man of no understanding. It is easy to act like him as a man of understanding, but it is not easy to imitate him in the way he showed how to act as a man of no understanding."

21. When Confucius in the last days of his travels abroad was in a certain State he was heard to say, " I must think of going home. I must really think of going home. My young people at home are all high-spirited and independent; they are, besides, accomplished in all the arts ; but they have no judgment."

22. Confucius, remarking of two ancient worthies, [22] famous for the purity and saintliness of their lives and character, said, " They forgave old wrongs : therefore they had little to complain of the world."

23. Confucius remarked of a character of the time, " Who says that the man is an honest man ? When

[22] The names of these two men are Pe-Yi and Shuh-Ts'i, who were two sons of a prince of a small principality. They both gave up their heirship to the throne to a younger brother and retired from the world. When the old Imperial dynasty was changed, they refused to eat the grain of the new dynasty, and finally starved themselves to death at the foot of a lonely mountain.

" Small is it that thou canst trample the Earth with its injuries under thy feet as Greek Zeno trained thee ; but thou canst love the Earth while it injures thee and even because it injures thee ; for this a greater than Zeno was needed, and he, too, was sent."

CARLYLE,—" Sartor Resartus."

somebody begged him for some household necessary, he went and begged of his neighbours for it and gave it as his own."

24. Confucius remarked, "Plausible speech, fine manners and studied earnestness are things of which a friend of mine was ashamed; I am also ashamed of such things. To conceal resentment against a person and to make friends with him : that is also something of which my same friend was ashamed ; I am also ashamed to do such a thing."

25. On one occasion, when two of his disciples, the favourite Yen Hui and Chung Yu the intrepid, were in attendance on him, Confucius said to them, "Now tell me, each of you, your aim in the conduct of life."

"I would like," answered the intrepid Chung Yu, "If I had carriages and horses and clothings of costly furs to share them with my friends, to be able to consider such things as much belonging to them as belonging to me."

"And I," answered the favourite, Yen Hui, "I would like to be able not to boast of my ability and to be able to be humble in my estimate of what I have done for others."

"Now," said the intrepid Chung Yu then to Confucius, "We would like to hear *your* aim, sir, in the conduct of life."

"My aim," replied Confucius, "would be to be a comfort to my old folk at home ; to be sincere, and to be found trustworthy by my friends ; and to love and care for my young people at home."

26. Confucius was once heard to say, "Alas ! I do not see now a man who can see his own failing or is willing to bring a suit against himself before his own conscience."

27. Confucius once remarked, "Even in a very small town there must be men who are as conscientious and honest as myself: only they have not tried to cultivate themselves as I have done."

CHAPTER VI.

1. Confucius, once expressing admiration for a disciple, remarked, "There is Yung—he should be made a prince."

On another occasion, when that disciple asked Confucius' opinion of a certain public character of the time, Confucius answered, "He is a good man : he is independent."

"But," replied the disciple, "when a man in his private life is serious with himself, he may, in his public life, be independent in dealing with the people. But to be independent with himself in his private life [2] as well as independent in his public life,—is there not too much independence in that ?" "Yes," answered Confucius, "you are right."

2. The reigning prince of Confucius' native State asked him which one of his disciples he considered a man of real culture.

---

[2] It is recorded of this character that he would strip himself, as many Chinese now do in summer, which led Confucius to say, "That is the way to lead men to forget the difference between a man and a beast,"

Confucius answered, " There was Yen Hui. He never made others suffer for his own annoyances. He never did a wrong thing twice. But unfortunately he died in the prime of his life. Now there is no one, none who can be said to be a man of real culture."

3. On one occasion when a disciple of Confucius was sent on a public mission to a foreign State, he left his mother at home unprovided for. Another disciple then asked Confucius to provide her with grain. "Give her," said Confucius, "so much," naming a certain quantity. The disciple asked for more. Confucius then named a larger quantity. Finally the disciple gave her a larger quantity than the quantity which Confucius named.

When Confucius came to know of it, he remarked, " When that woman's son left on his mission he drove in a carriage with fine horses and was clothed with costly furs. Now I believe a wise and good man reserves his charity for the really needy; he does not help the well-to-do and rich."

On another occasion, when another disciple was appointed the chief magistrate of a town, Confucius appointed his salary at nine hundred measures of grain. The disciple declined it as being too much.

"Do not decline it," said Confucius to him, "If that is more than necessary for your own wants, cannot you share what you do not want with your relatives and neighbours at home ?"

4. Confucius remarked of a disciple whose father was a notoriously bad man, saying : "The calf of a brindled cow, provided it be well conditioned, although men may hesitate to use it in sacrifice, is yet not unacceptable to the Spirits of the land."

5. A minister who was in power in Confucius' native State asked him if his disciple, the intrepid Chung Yu, could be made a minister under the government. "He is a man of decision," answered Confucius. "What is there in being a minister under the government that he should find any difficulty in it ?" The minister then put the same question with regard to another disciple. "He is a man of great penetration," answered Confucius. "What is there in being a minister that he should find any difficulty in it ?"

The minister then went on to ask the same question about another disciple. "He is a man of many accomplishments," answered Confucius. "What is there in being a minister that he should find any difficulty in it?"

6. Confucius remarked of his disciple, the favourite Yen Hui, saying, "For months he could live without

deviating from a pure moral life in thought as in deed. With other people, the utmost is a question of a day or a month."

7. A minister in power in Confucius' native State sent for a disciple of Confucius to make him the chief magistrate of an important town.

" Politely decline the offer for me," said the disciple to the messenger sent to him, "and if your master again should send for me, I shall have to leave the country altogether."

8. On one occasion, when a disciple was sick with an infectious disease, Confucius went to see him. Confucius, however, did not enter the house, but, taking the sick man's hands from outside the window, made him his last adieus. Confucius was then heard to say, " We shall lose him. But God's will be done!" At the same time he went on repeating, " Ah ! that such a man should die of such a sickness. Ah ! that such a man should die of such a sickness!"

9. Confucius remarked of his disciple, the favourite Yen Hui, saying, " How much heroism is in that man ! Living on one single meal a day, with water for his drink, and living in the lowest hovels of the city,—no man could have stood such hardships, yet he—he did not lose his cheerfulness. How much heroism is in that man!"

7

10. A disciple once said to Confucius, "It is not because I do not believe in your teaching, but I want the strength to carry it out into practice."

"Those," answered Confucius, "who only want the necessary strength, show it when they are on the way. But you—you stick at it from the outset altogether."

11. Confucius said to a disciple, "Be a good and wise man while you try to be an encyclopædic man of culture;²⁴ be not a fool while you try to be an encyclopædic man of culture."

12. On one occasion, when a disciple was appointed chief magistrate of an important town, Confucius said to him, "Have you succeeded in getting a good man under you?"

"Yes," answered the disciple, "I have now a man who would never act upon expediency. He never comes to see me in my house except when there is urgent public business to be done."

13. Confucius remarked of a chivalrous public character of the time, saying, "He was a man who never would boast. On one occasion, when the troops among whom he was, took to flight, he slowly brought

²⁴ Literally "a humanist,"—the term now used for a Confucianist and Confucianism.

"The aim in education," says Comenius, "is to teach him everything which is necessary to enable him to attain to what a human being can attain to."

up the rear; and when they had approached the city gate to which they were retreating, he whipped his horse and was the last man to enter the gate, remarking, simply, 'It was not courage which kept me behind. But you see—my horse would not go!'"

14. Confucius, referring to two noted characters of his time, remarked, "A man who has not the wit of that parson (the Sydney Smith of the time) and the fine appearance of that noble lord (the Lord Chesterfield of the time), will never get on in society now."

15. Confucius remarked, "Who can get out of the house except through the door. How is it that men do not know that one cannot live except through the Way?"[25]

16. Confucius remarked, "When the natural qualities of men get the better of the results of education, they are rude men. When the results of education get the better of their natural qualities, they become *literati.* It is only when the natural qualities and the results of education are properly blended, that we have the truly wise and good man."

17. Confucius remarked, "Man is born to be upright; when a man ceases to be that, it is by the merest chance that he can keep himself alive."

* Sine via, non itur.

18. Confucius remarked, "Those who know it are not as those who love it ; those who love it are not as those who find their joy in it." [26]

19. Confucius remarked, "You may speak of high things to those who in natural qualities of mind are above average men.   You may not speak to those who in natural qualities of mind are below average men."

20. A disciple enquired what constituted understanding.

Confucius answered, "To know the essential duties of man living in a society of men, and to hold in awe and fear the Spiritual Powers of the Universe, while keeping aloof from irreverent familiarity with them ; that may be considered as understanding."

The disciple then asked what constituted a moral life.

Confucius answered, "A man who wants to live a moral life must first be conscious within himself of a difficulty and has struggled to overcome the difficulty : that is the definition or test of a moral life."

---

[26] This is the difference between a moralist, a philosopher, and a real man of religion.

21. Confucius remarked, "Men of intellectual character delight in water scenery; men of moral character delight in mountain scenery. Intellectual men are active; moral men are calm. Intellectual men enjoy life; moral men live long."

22. Confucius, referring to the state of government in his native State and that in a neighbouring State, remarked, "If Ts'i[27] would only reform, she would have as good a government as Lu (Confucius' native State), and if Lu would only reform she would have a perfect government."

23. Confucius was once heard to exclaim, "A goblet that is not globular: why call it a goblet; why call it a goblet?"[28]

24. A disciple of Confucius once said to him, "A moral man,—if somebody told him that there was a man fallen into a well, I suppose he would immediately follow into the well?"

[27] An Englishman would perhaps say the France of ancient feudal China: noted for chivalry, *disinterestedness* and love of ideas in the character of her people; but at Confucius' time, given too much over to false Liberalism. Lu (Confucius' native State) was perhaps the England or Great Britain of ancient China: noted for love of morality and common sense in the character of her people, but inaptness for ideas which made them rather utilitarian in their politics and government. Both States were in the modern province of Shantung, on the sea-coast.

[28] Referring to an article of common use then which had become a misnomer, and to many things; especially, many kinds of -isms and -ities in Confucius' time which had also become misnomers.

"Why should he?" replied Confucius, "A good and wise man might be led to hurry to the scene, but not to plunge into the well. He could be imposed upon, but not made a fool of."

25. Confucius remarked, "A good man who studies extensively into the arts and literature, and directs his studies with judgment and taste, is not likely to get into a wrong track."

26. On one occasion when Confucius allowed himself to be presented to a princess of a State who was notorious for the irregularities of her life, his disciple, the intrepid Chung Yu, was vexed.

Confucius then swore an oath, saying, "If I have had an unworthy motive in doing that, may God forsake me—may God forsake me for ever!"

27. Confucius remarked, "The use of the moral sentiment, well balanced and kept in perfect equilibrium,—that is the true state of human perfection. It is seldom found long so kept up amongst man."

28. A disciple once said to Confucius, "If there is a man who carries out extensively good works for the welfare of the people and is really able to benefit the multitude what would you say of such a man: could he be called a moral character?"

"Why call him only a moral character," answered Confucius, "if one must call such a man by a name, one would call him a holy or sainted man. For, judged by the works of which you speak, even the ancient Emperors Yao and Shun* felt their shortcomings."

29. Confucius remarked, "A moral man in forming his character forms the character of others; in enlightening himself he enlightens others. It is a good method in attaining a moral life, if one is able to consider how one would see things and act if placed in the position of others."

---

* The Abraham and Isaac in patriarchal times of Chinese history.

MENCIUS, making use of these names to illustrate his teaching, says : "A man rises early every morning and works persistently all day long, for what? For righteousness: then he is a son of Abraham (Shun). Another man also rises early every morning and works persistently all day long, for what? For gain: then he is a son of Barabbas the Robber. (盜 跖.)

❣

CHAPTER VII.

1. Confucius remarked, "I transmit the old truth and do not originate any new theory. I am well acquainted and love the study of Antiquity. In this respect I may venture to compare myself with our old Worthy Pang.⁎"

2. Confucius then went on to say, "To meditate in silence ; patiently to acquire knowledge ; and to be indefatigable in teaching it to others: which one of these things can I say that I have done ?"

3. Lastly, Confucius said, "Neglect of godliness ; study without understanding ; failure to act up to what I believe to be right ; and inability to change bad habits : these are things which cause me constant solicitude."

4. But notwithstanding what he said above, Confucius in his disengaged hours was always serene and cheerful.

5. Only once in his old age Confucius was heard to say : "How my mental powers have decayed !   For a

⁎ A famous antiquarian of the time.

long time now I have not dreamt, as I was wont to do, of our Lord of Chou.[31] "

6. Confucius said to his disciples : "Seek for wisdom ; hold fast to godliness ; live a moral life ; and enjoy the pleasures derived from the pursuit of the polite arts."

7. Confucius remarked, "In teaching men, I make no difference between the rich and the poor. I have taught men who could just afford to bring me the barest presentation gift in the same way as I have taught others."

8. Confucius then went on to say : "In my method of teaching, I always wait for my student to make an effort himself to find his way through a difficulty, before I show him the way myself. I also make him find his own illustrations before I give him one of my own. When I have pointed out the bearing of a subject in one direction and found that my student cannot himself see its bearings into other directions, I do not then repeat my lesson."

9. When Confucius dined in a house of mourning he never ate much. On the same day in which he had

---

[31] The Moses or Solon of Chinese History : the Founder also of Confucius' native State, Lu (the England of Ancient China) ; a man who combined the piety of St. Augustine and the statesmanship of King Alfred of England.

occasion to mourn for the death of a friend, the sound of music was never heard in his house.

10. Confucius once said to his disciple, the favourite Yen Hui, "To act when called upon to act, in public life, and, when neglected, to be content to lead out a private life :—that is what you and I—we both have made up our minds upon."

When his other disciple, the intrepid Chung Yu, heard the remark, he said to Confucius : "But if you were in command of an army, whom would you have with you ?"

"I would not have him," replied Confucius, "who is ready to seize a live tiger with his bare arms, or jump into the sea, without fear of death. The man I would have with me would be a man who is conscious of the difficulties of any task set before him, and who, only after mature deliberation, proceeds to accomplish it."

11. Confucius once remarked, "If there is a sure way of getting rich, even though one had to be a groom and keep horses, I would be willing to be one. But as there is really no sure way of getting rich, I prefer to follow the pursuits congenial to me."

12. There were three cases in life in which Confucius considered a man was called upon to exercise the

most mature deliberation : in case of worship, of war and of sickness.

13. When Confucius on his travels was in a certain State he, for the first time, heard played a piece of ancient music (the oldest then known in China)." Thereupon he gave himself up to the study of it for three months, to the entire neglect of his ordinary food. He was then heard to say, " I should never have thought that music could be brought to such perfection."

14. A disciple who was with Confucius on his travels while in a certain State,—speaking of the reigning prince of that State who, while his father was driven to exile, succeeded, on his grandfather's death, to the throne, and was then opposing the attempt of his father to return to the country,—said to another disciple : "Is the master in favour of the son, the present ruler?" "Oh," replied the other disciple, " I will ask him."

The other disciple accordingly went in where Confucius was, and said to him : "What kind of men were Po-yi and Shuh-ts'i?" " "They are ancient worthies," answered Confucius. "But," asked the disciple, "did they complain of the world?" "No," replied Confucius, "what they sought for in life was to live a high moral life, and they succeeded in living a high moral life. What had they then to complain of the world?" The disciple then went out and said to the other disciple, "No, the master is not in favour of the present ruler."

15. Confucius remarked, "Living upon the poorest fare with cold water for drink, and with my bended arms for a pillow,—I could yet find pleasure in such a life, whereas riches and honours acquired through the sacrifice of what is right, would be to me as unreal as a mirage."

16. Confucius once remarked, after he had begun the study of the I-king,³⁴ "If I could hope to live some years more, long enough to complete my study of the I-king, I should then hope to be without any great shortcomings in my life."

17. The subjects upon which Confucius loved to talk were: Poetry, history, and the rules of courtesy and good manners. He frequently talked on these subjects.

18. The reigning prince of a small principality asked a disciple of Confucius, the intrepid Chung Yu, to

³⁴ This book is now known to foreigners as "The Book of Changes," one of the so-called five Classics in the Chinese Bible. It *seems*, to us, the book is an attempt at a mathematical or exact scientific statement of mental phenomena and moral problems. It might be called, "The Theory of Fluxions," applied originally to the actions of physical forces in nature, but now, as it stands,—to the moral forces and intellectual forces in the world. Sir CHALONER ALABASTER has published the only intelligible papers on this book, which should be consulted by anyone interested in the subject.

give his opinion of Confucius.   The disciple did not say anything in reply.   When Confucius afterwards heard of the enquiry, he said to his disciple : "Why did you not say to him thus : 'He is a man who, in the efforts he makes to overcome the difficulty in acquiring knowledge, neglects his food, and, in the joy of its attainment, forgets his sorrows of life ; and, who thus absorbed, becomes oblivious that old age is stealing on him ?'"

19. Confucius remarked, "I am not one born with understanding.   I am only one who has given himself to the study of Antiquity and is diligent in seeking for understanding in such studies.

20. Confucius always refused to talk of supernatural phenomena ; of extraordinary feats of strength ; of crime or unnatural depravity of men; or of supernatural beings.

21. Confucius remarked, "When three men meet together, one of them who is anxious to learn can always learn something of the other two.   He can profit by the good example of the one and avoid the bad example of the other."

22. Confucius, on one occasion of great personal danger to his person from an enemy, was heard to say, "God has given me this moral and intellectual power in me ; what can that man do to me ?"

23. But on another occasion Confucius remarked to his disciples, " Do you think, my friends, that I have some mysterious power within me ? I have really nothing mysterious in me,—to you, of all others. For if there is anyone who shows to you everything which he does, I am, you know, my friends, that person."

24. Confucius through his life and teaching taught only four things : a knowledge of literature and the arts, conduct, conscientiousness and truthfulness.

25. Confucius once, speaking of the men and state of the society of his time, remarked, "Holy, sainted men I do not expect to see ; if I could only meet with wise and good men I would be satisfied.

" Perfectly honest men I do not expect to see ; if I could only meet with scrupulous men I would be satisfied. But in a state of society in which men must pretend to possess what they really do not possess ; pretend to have plenty, when they have really nothing ; and pretend to be in affluence when they are in actual want :—in such a state of society, it is difficult to be even a scrupulous man."

26. Confucius sometimes went out fishing, but always with the rod and angle ; he would never use a net. He sometimes went out shooting, but he would never shoot at a bird except on the wing.

27. Confucius once remarked, "There are, perhaps, men who propound theories which they themselves do not understand. That is a thing I never do. I read and learn everything and, choosing what is excellent, I adopt it; I see everything and take note of what I see: that is, perhaps, next to having a great understanding."

28. A certain place was noted for the bad character of the people in it. When Confucius allowed a young man of that place to be presented to him, his disciples were astonished. But Confucius said, "Why should one be too severe? When a man reforms and comes to me for advice, I accept his present reformation without inquiring what his past life has been. I am satisfied if I find that, for the present, he has really reformed, without being able to guarantee that he will not relapse again. But why should one be too severe?"

29. Confucius then went on to remark, "Is moral life something remote or difficult? If a man will only wish to live a moral life — there and then his life becomes moral."

30. A minister of justice in a certain State enquired of Confucius, while he was in that State on his travels, if the reigning prince in Confucius' native State was a

man of propriety in his life. "Yes," answered Confucius, "he is."

After a while, when Confucius had left, the minister beckoned to a disciple of Confucius to approach, and said to him : "I have always been taught to believe that a good and wise man is impartial in his judgment. But now I find it is not so. The reigning prince of your State married a princess from the reigning house of a State whose family surname is the same as that of your prince ; and, to conceal the impropriety,[18] your prince changed her surname in the title given to her at Court. Now if, after this, your prince can be considered a man of propriety in life, who may not be considered so ?"

Afterwards when the disciple told Confucius of what the minister said, Confucius remarked, "I am glad that whenever I make a mistake, people always know it."

31. When Confucius asked a man to sing, if he sang well, Confucius would make him sing again the same song, accompanying him with his own voice.

32. Confucius remarked, "In the knowledge of letters and the arts, I may perhaps compare myself with

---

[18] It was and is considered very improper in China for a man to marry not only a first cousin, but even a woman whose same family surname with himself, might prove her to be a distant first cousin.

other men. But as for the character of a good and wise man who carries out in his personal conduct what he professes,—that is something to which I have not yet attained."

33. Confucius then went on to say, "And as for the character of a holy, sainted man or even a moral character,—how should I dare even to pretend to that. That I spare no pains in striving after it and am indefatigable in teaching others to strive for it,— that, perhaps, may be said of me."

A disciple, who heard what was said, thereupon remarked, "That is where we, your disciples, cannot follow you."

34. On one occasion when Confucius was sick, a disciple asked that he would allow prayers to be offered for his recovery. "Is it the custom?" asked Confucius. "Yes," replied the disciple, "in the Book of Rituals for the Dead it is written, 'Pray to the Powers above and pray to the Powers below.'"

"Ah," said Confucius then, "my prayer has been a long—lifelong—one."

35. Confucius remarked, "Extravagance leads to

9

excess ; thrift to meanness : but it is better to be mean than to be guilty of excess." [36]

36. Confucius remarked, " A wise and good man is composed and happy ; a fool is always worried and full of distress."

37. Confucius, in his look, was gracious but serious[37]; he was awe-inspiring but not austere ; he was earnest but unaffected.

---

[36] Sir CHALONER ALABASTER translates : " Extravagance leads to sin ; thrift makes men mean : but it is better to be mean than to sin."

[37] Beseligend war ihre Nähe,
Und alle Herzen wurden weit
Doch eine Würde, eine Höhe
Entfernt die Vertraulichkeit.
        Das Mädchen aus dem Fremde.—SCHILLER.

CHAPTER VIII.

1. Confucius speaking of a remote Founder of the Imperial House of Chou,[38] the then ruling dynasty, remarked: "He was a man, it may be said, of the highest moral greatness. He three times refused the government of the Empire; although the world, not knowing this, does not speak much of him."

2. Confucius remarked, "Earnestness without judgment becomes pedantry; caution without judgment becomes timidity; courage without judgment leads to crime; uprightness without judgment makes men tyrannical.

When the gentlemen of a country are attached to the members of their own family, the people will improve in their moral character;[39] when the gentlemen do not discard their old connections, the people will not become grasping in their character.

3. When a disciple of Confucius was on his death-bed, he called to him his own disciples and said to

---

[38] B.C. 1122-225.

[39] That is why the Scotch, who despise a kinless loon, are a peculiarly moral people.

them : "Uncover my feet ; uncover my hands. The
Psalm says :—

> 'Walk with fear and with trembling
>   As on the brink of a gulf ;
> For the ground you are treading
>   Is with thin ice covered above.'

But now, my young friends, I shall from henceforth
be free from all these things."

4. On the same occasion as mentioned above,
when a young noble of the Court came to see him,
the disciple said to him, "When the bird is dying, its
song is sad ; when a man is dying, his words are true.

"Now a gentleman in his education should consider
three things as essential. In his manners, he aspires
to be free from excitement and familiarity. In the
expression of his countenance, he seeks to inspire
confidence. In the choice of his language, he aims at
freedom from vulgarity and unreasonableness. As to
the knowledge of the technical details of the arts and
sciences, he leaves that to professional men."

5. A disciple of Confucius remarked, "Gifted
himself, yet seeking to learn from the ungifted ;
possessing much information himself, yet seeking it
from others possessing less ; rich himself in the treasures
of his mind, yet appearing as though he were poor ;

profound himself, yet appearing as though he were superficial:—I once had a friend who thus spent his life."

6. A disciple of Confucius remarked, " A man who could be depended upon when the life of an orphan prince, his master's child, is entrusted to his care, or the safety of a kingdom is confided to his charge,—who will not, in any great emergency of life and death, betray his trust,—such a man I would call a gentleman; such a man I would call a perfect gentleman."

7. A disciple of Confucius remarked, "An educated gentleman may not be without strength and resoluteness of character. His responsibility in life is a heavy one, and the way is long. He is responsible to himself for living a moral life; is that not a heavy responsibility? He must continue in it until he dies; is the way then not a long one?"

8. Confucius remarked, "In education sentiment is called out by the study of poetry;[40] judgment is formed by the study of the arts; and education of the character is completed by the study of music."

---

* WORDSWORTH says of poetry that it tends to :—
    " Nourish the imagination in her growth,
    And give the mind that apprehensive power,
    Whereby she is made quick to recognise
    The moral properties and scope of things."

9. Confucius remarked, "The common people should be educated in what they ought to do ; not to ask why they should do it." [41]

10. Confucius remarked, "A man of courage who hates to be poor will be sure to commit a crime. A man without moral character, if too much hated, will also be sure to commit a crime."

11. Confucius remarked, "A man may have abilities as admirable as our Lord of Chou, [42] but if he is proud and mean, you need not consider the other qualities of his mind."

12. Confucius remarked, "A man who educates himself for three years without improvement is seldom to be found."

13. Confucius remarked, "A man who is scrupulously truthful, cultured and steadfast to the death in the path of honesty, [43] such a man should not serve in a country where the government is in a state of revolution

[41] A Chinese commentator, Ch'eng, of the Sung dynasty, says here: "Confucius said this not because he did not wish the people to understand, but because it is impossible to make them understand. But if you say Confucius did not *wish* the people to understand, that would mean that he would govern the people by jugglery or Jesuitism, as is sometimes done by later generations,—a supposition which is preposterous."

GOETHE, in his latter years, was inclined to believe that Martin Luther put back the civilisation of Europe because he appealed to the multitude to judge of things which they could not possibly be in a position to understand. The real and true principle of modern democracy, on the other hand, is contained in that saying of Confucius :—

"Greatly fear the aspirations (the inarticulate, not the mere articulate aspirations) of the people" 大畏民志.

[42] The Moses or Solon of Chinese History [*see* note Chapter VII, Section 5.]

[43] Like the late General Charles (Chinese) Gordon.

nor live in a country where the government is in an actual state of anarchy. When there is justice and order in the government of the world, he should be known, but when there is no justice and order in the government of the world he should be obscure. When there is justice and order in the government of his own country, he should be ashamed to be poor and without honour ; but when there is no justice in the government of his own country he should be ashamed to be rich and honoured."

14. Confucius remarked, " A man who is not in office in the government of a country, should never give advice as to its policy."

15. Confucius speaking of the performance of a great musician of the time remarked, "The volume of sound at the commencement and the clash and commingling of harmony at the end of that ancient ballad he played were magnificent. How it seemed to fill the ears ! "

16. Confucius remarked, "Appearance of high spirit without integrity ; of dullness without humility ; of simplicity without honesty ;—of such men I really do not know what to say."

17. Confucius remarked, " In education study

always as if you have not yet reached your goal and as though apprehensive of losing it."

18. Confucius remarked, " How toweringly high and surpassingly great in moral grandeur was the way by which the ancient Emperors Shun and Yü came to the government of the Empire, and yet they themselves were unconscious of it." [44]

19. Confucius remarked, "Oh! how great, as a ruler of men, was Yao [45] the Emperor! Ah! how toweringly high and surpassingly great: Yao's moral greatness is comparable only to the greatness of God. How vast and infinite : the people had no name for such moral greatness. How surpassingly great he was in the works he accomplished! How glorious he was in the arts he established."

20. The great Emperor Shun had five great Public Servants and the Empire had peace. King Wu [46] said, " I had ten great Public Servants who assisted me in restoring order in the Empire."

Confucius, remarking on the above, observed : " It

[44] The Isaac and Jacob of Chinese history : two men in early patriarchic times in China who rose from the ploughshare to the throne. [B.C. 2255-2205 and B.C. 2205-2197.]

[45] The Abraham of Chinese history. [B.C. 2356-2258.]

[46] The warrior king or the conqueror : the Solomon of Chinese history. [B.C. 1122-1115.]

was said of old that men of great ability are difficult to find. The saying is very true. The great men who lived during the period between the reigns of T'ang (the title of the Emperor Yao) and Yü (the title of Shun) have never been equalled. Among the ten great Public Servants mentioned above, there was one woman : so that there were really only nine great men.

"The House of Chou then had two-thirds of the Empire under them, while still acknowledging the sovereignty of the House of Yin. The moral greatness of the early Emperors of the House of Chou may be considered perfect.

21. Confucius remarked, "I have not been able to find a flaw in the character of the ancient Emperor, the Great Yü.[47] He was extremely simple in his own food and drink, but lavish in what he offered in sacrifice. His ordinary clothing was coarse and poor, but when he went to worship he appeared in rich and appropriate robes. The palace where he lived was humble and mean, but he spared no expense in useful public works for the good of the people. In all this I cannot find a flaw in the character of the Great Yü!"

[47] *See* note 44, Section 18 of this Chapter.

10

CHAPTER IX.

1. Confucius in his conversation seldom spoke of interests, of religion or of morality.

2. A man of a certain place remarked, "Confucius is certainly a great man. He is a man of very extensive acquirements, but he has not distinguished himself in anything so as to make himself a name."

When Confucius heard of the remark, he said to his disciples, "Now what shall I take up to distinguish myself? Shall I take up driving or shall I take up archery? I think I will take up archery."

3. Confucius remarked, "Linen hats were considered good taste, but now people generally wear silk ones. The latter are less expensive; therefore I follow the general practice. It was considered correct form at one time to make your bow, as you enter, from the lower part of the room; but now the practice is to make your bow from the upper end of the room. The latter practice presumes too much; therefore I continue to make my bow from the lower part of the room."

4. There were four things from which Confucius
was entirely free : He was free from self-interest, from
prepossessions, from bigotry and from egoism.

5. On one occasion, when Confucius was in fear
for his personal safety from the violence of men of a
certain place, he said to those about him, " Be not
afraid. Since the death of King Wan [who founded
this civilisation] is not the cause of this civilisation with
us here now ? If God is going to destroy all civilisation
in the world, it would not have been given to a mortal
of this late generation to understand this civilisation.
But if God is not going to destroy all civilisation in
the world—what can the people of this place do to
me ? "

6. A minister of a certain State asked a disciple
of Confucius, saying : Your teacher—he is a holy man,
is he not ? What a variety of acquirements he seems to
possess." The disciple replied, " God has certainly
been bountiful to him to make him a holy man.
Besides he has himself acquired knowledge in many
things."

When Confucius afterwards heard of the conversation, he remarked, " Does the minister know me ?
When I was young, I was in a low position in life :
therefore I had to acquire knowledge in many things ;

but they were merely ordinary matters of routine. You think a wise and good man requires much knowledge to make him so; no, he does not require much."

A disciple also once remarked, "I have heard the Master say : ' I have not been called to act in public life ; therefore I have had time to acquaint myself with many arts.' "

7. Confucius once remarked to someone, "Do you think I have a great understanding? I have no great understanding at all. When an ordinary person asks my opinion on a subject, I myself have no opinion whatever of the subject; but by asking questions on the pros and cons, I get to the bottom of it.

8. Confucius was once heard to exclaim, "Ah, woe 's me. I do not see any signs either in heaven or on earth that we are near the end of the present period of disorder and anarchy and that we are about to inaugurate a new order of things in the world."

9. When Confucius met a person dressed in deep mourning, an officer in full uniform or a blind person, on their approach, although such persons were younger than himself, he would always stand up, and, when walking past them, he would respectfully quicken his steps."

10. A disciple, the favourite Yen Hui, speaking in admiration of Confucius' teaching, remarked : "The more I have looked up to it the higher it appears. The more I have tried to penetrate into it the more impenetrable it seems to be. When I have thought I have laid hold of it here, lo ! it is there. But the Master knows admirably how to lead people on step by step. He has enlarged my mind with an extensive knowledge of the arts, while guiding and correcting my judgment and taste. Thus I could not stop in my progress, even if I would. But when I have exhausted my efforts and thought I have reached it, the goal would still stand clear and distinct away from me, and I have no means of reaching it, make what efforts I will."

11. On one occasion, when Confucius was seriously sick, his disciple, the intrepid Chung Yu, made arrangements, in case of the decease of the sick man, that each of the disciples should assume the function of an officer in the household of a great noble. When Confucius came to know of what the disciple did, he, in a remission of his sickness, remarked : I have for this long while observed that Yu (Chung Yu) practises self-deception in his actions. To pretend to have public officers when I have none : whom do I want to

impose upon by that? Do I want to impose upon God? Besides, is it not better that I should die in the arms of you, my friends, than in the arms of mere unsympathetic officers? Again, even if I should never be buried with the honours of a public funeral, am I likely to be left unburied on the public road?"

12. A disciple once said to Confucius, "There is a beautiful gem here. Shall I put it in a case and lay it by ; or shall I seek for a good price and sell it ?"

"Sell it by all means," answered Confucius, "Sell it by all means ; but, if I were you, I should wait until the price were offered."

13. On one occasion Confucius said he would go and live among the barbarous tribes in the East. "You will there," remarked somebody, "feel the want of refinement."

"Where a wise and good man lives," replied Confucius, "there will be no want of refinement."

14. Confucius remarked, "When I finally returned from my travels, to my native State, I completed my work of reforming the State Music and arranging the Songs and Psalms in the Book of Ballads, Songs and Psalms, assigning each piece to its proper place in the book."

15. Confucius remarked, "In public life to do one's duty to the nobles and princes whom one serves under; in private life to do one's duty to the members of one's family; in performing the last offices to the dead, to spare no pains lest anything should be neglected; and in using wine, to be able to resist the temptation of taking it to excess;—which one of these things can I say that I have been able to do?"

16. Confucius once standing by a stream, remarked, "How all things in nature are passing away even like this,—ceasing neither day nor night!"

17. Confucius once remarked, "I do not now see a man who can love moral worth in man as he loves beauty in woman."

18. Confucius remarked, "Suppose a man wants to raise a mound* and, just as it wants only one basket more of earth to complete the work, suppose he were suddenly to stop: the stopping depends entirely upon himself. Suppose again a man wants to level a road,

*Life lies before us as a huge quarry lies before the architect. He deserves not the name of architect except when, out of this fortuitous mass of materials, he can combine with the greatest economy, fitness and durability, some form the pattern of which originated in his own spirit. . . . Believe me, most part of the misery and mischief, of all that is denominated evil in this world, arises from the fact that men are too remiss to get a proper knowledge of their aims, and, when they do get it, to work persistently in attaining them. They seem to me like people who have taken up a notion that they must and will erect a tower, but who yet expend on the foundation not more stones and labour than would be sufficient for a hut."—GOETHE, *Wilhelm Meister.*

although he has just thrown over it only one basket of earth ; to proceed with the work also depends entirely upon himself."

19. Confucius remarked of his disciple, the favourite Yen Hui : "He was the only man who was never tired and inattentive while I talked with him."

20. Confucius remarked of the same disciple : "Alas! he is dead. I have observed his constant advance ; I never saw him stop in his progress."

21. Confucius once, speaking of the career of his many disciples, remarked : Some only sprout up, but do not flower ; some only flower, but do not ripen into fruit."

22. Confucius remarked, "Youths should be respected. How do we know that their future will not be as good as we are now? Only when a man is forty or fifty without having done anything to distinguish himself, does he then cease to command respect."

23. Confucius remarked, "If you speak to a man in the strict words of the law, he will probably agree with you ; but the important point is that he should so profit by what you say to him as to change his conduct. If you speak to a man in parables, he will probably be pleased with your story ; but the important point is that he should apply the moral to himself. Now when I find

a man who agrees with me in what I say, without being able so to profit by it as to change his conduct, or one who is pleased with my parable without being able to apply the moral to himself,—I can do nothing for such a man."

24. Confucius remarked, "Make conscientiousness and sincerity your first principles. Have no friends who are not as yourself. When you have bad habits do not hesitate to change them."[*]

25. Confucius remarked, "The general of an army may be carried off, but a man of the common people cannot be robbed of his free will."

26. Confucius remarked of his disciple, the intrepid Chung Yu, "Dressed in an old shabby suit of russet cloth and standing among a crowd dressed in costly furs without being ashamed,—that is Yu! (the disciple's familiar name):—

> . "Without envy, without greed,
> What he does is good indeed."

Afterwards, when the intrepid Chung Yu kept repeating those two lines of poetry, Confucius remarked, "That alone is not good indeed."

* Repetition of Chapter I, Section 8.

11

27. Confucius remarked, "When the cold of winter comes, it is then you know that the pine tree and the cypress are the last to lose their green."[50]

28. Confucius remarked, "Men of intelligence are free from doubts, moral men from anxiety, and men of courage from fear."

29. Confucius remarked, "Some men there are with whom you can share your knowledge of *facts*, but who cannot follow you in arriving at *principles*. Some can follow you to *particular* principles, but they cannot arrive with you at *general* principles. Some can arrive with you at general principles but they cannot apply the general principles under exceptional circumstances."

30. How they are waving, waving,
The blossoming myrtles gay;
Do I not think of you, love?
Your home is far away.

Confucius, repeating those lines, remarked, "That is because men do not think. Why is it far away?"

[50] Scilicet ut fulvum spectatur in ignibus aurum,
Tempore sic duro est adspicienda fides.
OVID.

[51] Ein sanfter Wind vom blauen Himmel weht,
Die Myrte still und hoch der Lorbeer steht,
Kennst du es wohl? Dahin! Dahin,
Möcht' ich mit dir, O mein Geliebter, ziehn.—GOETHE.

But the Ideal—our America, as the young man in *Wilhelm Meister* says,—is *here* in the present, *actual*, and not far away.

CHAPTER X.

1. Confucius in his life at home was shy and diffident, as if he were not a good speaker. In public life, however, in courts and councils, he spoke readily, but with deliberation.

2. At court, in conversation with the junior officers, he spoke with frankness; with the senior officers, he spoke with self-possession.

In the presence of his prince, he looked diffident, awe-inspired, but composed.

3. When his prince called to him to see a visitor out, he would start up with attention, make obeisance to receive the command; then, bowing right and left to officers in attendance and adjusting the folds of his robes, he would quicken his step, and walk out, not stiffly, but with dignity and ease. When the visitor had left, he would return to his place, announcing simply, " The guest has retired."

4. In entering the rooms of the palace, he would bend low his body at the door as if it were not high enough to admit him. In the room he would never

stand right before the door, nor, in entering it, step on the door sill.

In passing into the Presence Chamber, he would start up with attention and speak only in whispers. Then, holding up the folds of his robes, he would ascend the steps leading to the throne, bending low his body and holding in his breath as if he were afraid to breathe.

After the audience, when he had descended one step away from the throne, he would relax his countenance and assume his ordinary look. After clearing the last steps, he would quicken his pace and walk with ease and dignity to resume his place among the courtiers, looking diffident, with awe and attention.

5. When he had to carry the sceptre of the prince, he would bend low his body as if the weight were too heavy for him ; holding it not higher than his forehead nor lower than his chest, and, with his look all awe and attention, walk with slow, measured steps.

At a public reception in the foreign courts to which he was sent, he behaved with great dignity. At a private audience in such courts, he was genial and engaging in his manners.

6. Confucius considered the following details necessary for a gentlemen to observe in matters of dress :—

A gentleman should never permit anything crimson or scarlet in colour to be seen in any part of his dress ; even in his underclothing he should avoid anything red or of a reddish colour.

In summer, when dressed in a single suit of gauze or grass-cloth, he should always wear something underneath, worn next to the skin. In winter he should line a black suit with lambskin ; a light suit with fawn skin ; a yellow suit with fox skin. His fur underclothing should be made long, with the right sleeve a little short.

He should always have a change of night-dress, which should be as long again as the trunk of his body.

When at home in winter, he should be dressed in a suit of fox or badger skin. When not in mourning, he may have any ornaments or appendages on the girdle of his dress. His under-garment, except when it is worn as an apron (like the Free Masons now) on State occasions, he should always have cut pointed on the upper part.

On a visit of condolence he should never wear a suit of lamb's fur or a dark blue hat. On the first day of the month he should always put on his full uniform when he goes to Court.

7. On days when he fasts and gives himself up to prayer, he should always put on a bright clean suit of plain cloth. On such days he should always change the ordinary articles of his food, and move out of his usual sitting-room.

8. The following are the details which Confucius observed in matters of food and eating :—

In his food, he liked to have the rice finely cleaned and the meat, when stewed, cut in small pieces. Rice injured by damp and heat, or turned sour, he would not take ; nor fish or flesh which was gone. He would not take anything that had an unwholesome colour or unwholesome flavour ; nor any articles of food which had been spoilt in cooking ; nor anything out of its season. Meat not properly cut he would not take ; nor any dish served without its proper sauce.

Although there might be plenty of meat on the table, he would never allow the quantity of meat he took to exceed a due proportion to the rice he took. It was only in wine that he did not set himself a limit ; but he never took it to excess.

He would not take wine or meat bought where it had been exposed for sale. He would always have ginger served on the table. He never ate much,

After a public sacrifice, he would never keep the portion of meat he received over night. The meat he used in sacrifice at home he would never keep over three days; if kept over three days, he would not allow it to be eaten.

At table, while eating, he would not speak. When in bed he would not talk.

Although he might have the plainest fare on the table, he would always say grace[12] before he ate.

9. In ordinary life, unless the mat used as a cushion was properly and squarely laid, he would not sit on it.[13]

10. When at a public dinner in his native place, he would always leave the table as soon as the old people left.

In his native place on the occasion of the Purification Festival, when the procession of villagers passed his house, he would always appear in full uniform on the steps of his house, standing on the left-hand side of the house.[14]

[12] An ancient Custom in China equivalent in meaning but not exactly the same as the "saying grace" in Europe. This custom is, I am told, observed in some country places in China to this day. The saying grace consists in setting aside a very small portion of the rice or meat on the table and offering it to the Powers to which the offrant is thankful that he has it to eat.

[13] In ancient China, as now in Japan, among the people, there were no chairs; people, even kings and princes, sat on mats on the floor.

[14] In old China and in most Eastern countries, sanitation forms a part of religion, not enforced by police or gens d'armes.

11. When he had occasion to entrust a message of enquiry after the health of a friend in another country to any person, he would always, on the person entrusted with the message leaving him, make obeisance twice and see him to the door.

On one occasion when a noble, who was the minister in power in his native State, sent him a present of some medicines, he received it respectfully, but said to the messenger : " Tell your Master I do not know the nature of the drugs : therefore I shall be afraid to use it."   .

12. On one occasion when, as he was returning from an audience at the palace, he heard that the State stable was on fire, his first question was, " Has any man been injured?" He did not ask about the horses.

13. When his prince sent him a present of a dish of cooked meat, he would always have it properly served on the table, and he himself would taste it before he allowed others to taste it. When his prince sent him uncooked meat as a present, he would have it cooked and then offer it first in sacrifice before his ancestors. When his prince sent him a live animal, he would keep it alive.

When he had the honour to sit with his prince at table, after the prince had said grace he would first taste the dishes.

When he was sick, on his prince coming to see him, he would lie with his head to the east and have his court uniform laid over him with the girdle drawn across.

When he received a summons from his prince he would immediately go on foot, without waiting for his carriage.

14. When he attended the service at the Great Cathedral (ancestral temple of the reigning prince) he always enquired what he should do at every stage of the service.

15. When any friend died who had no one to perform the last offices, he would always say : "Leave it to me : I will bury him."

When friends sent him presents, although these might consist of carriages and horses, he would not on receiving them make obeisance. The only present which he received with an obeisance was meat which had been used in sacrifice.

16. In bed, he was never seen to lie straight on his back like a corpse. In ordinary life at home, he would never use formality.

12

When he met anyone dressed in deep mourning, although the person might be a familiar acquaintance, he would always look grave and serious. When he met with an officer in full uniform or a blind person, although he himself might be in undress, he would always behave with ceremony and punctiliousness.

When driving in his carriage, on meeting with a funeral cortege, he would always bend his head forward out of the carriage, to bow. He would behave in the same way when he met the procession carrying the mortality returns of the population.

At a dinner, whenever a dish *en grand tenue* was brought to the table, he would look serious and rise up to thank the host.

On a sudden clap of thunder or during a violent storm, he would look grave and serious.

17. When about to mount his carriage he would stand in a proper position, holding the cord in his hand. When in the carriage he would look straight before him without turning his head. He would not talk fast or point with his fingers.

18. As they turned to look at it, it instantly rose and, hovering about, it settled again. Somebody said, "Ah ! pheasant on the hill ! Ah ! pheasant on the hill ! You know the times ! You know the times !" Confucius'

disciple, the intrepid Chung Yu, conned it over three times; then, suddenly understanding the meaning of the remark, made an exclamation, rose, and went away. [55]

[55] Chinese commentators give up the passage in this section, confessing they cannot understand its meaning. Sir CHALONER ALABASTER, however, has discovered a very good explanation of this passage which unfortunately we cannot exactly remember. We here make a guess of his explanation from memory.

CHAPTER XI.

1. Confucius remarked, "Men of the last generation, in matters of the arts and refinement, are considered to have been rude ; men of the present generation are, in those matters, considered polite. But in my practice I prefer men of the last generation."

2. Confucius in his old age remarked, "Of all those who followed me and shared hardships with me in my wanderings in former years, I do not now see one at my door.

"Distinguished for godliness and conduct there were Yen Hui, Min Tzu Ch'ien, Jen Pih-niu and Chung Kung ; distinguished as good speakers there were Tsai Ngo and Tzu Kung ; for administrative abilities, Jen Yu and Chung Yu ; and for literary pursuits, Tzu Yu and Tzu Hsia."

3. Confucius remarked of his disciple, the favourite Yen Hui : "There was Hui—(the disciple's familiar name), he never gave me any assistance at all. There was nothing in what I said to him with which he was not satisfied."

4. Confucius remarked of another disciple, saying: "He was indeed a good son. People found nothing in him different from what his parents said of him."

5. A disciple of Confucius was fond of repeating the verse :—

> " A fleck on the stone may be ground away ;
> A word misspoken will remain alway."

Confucius married his niece to him.

6. A noble who was the minister in power in Confucius' native State, asked him which one of his disciples he considered a man of real culture.

Confucius answered, "There was Yen Hui; he was a man of real culture. But unfortunately he died in the prime of his life. Now there is no one like him."

7. When the favourite Yen Hui died, his father begged that Confucius would sell his carriage to buy an outer case for the coffin in which to bury him.

Confucius answered, "Talented or without talents, a man's son will always be to him as no other man's son. When my own son died, he was buried in a simple coffin without the outer case. Now I cannot go on foot to buy a coffin case for your son. As I have the honour to sit in the State Council of the country I am not permitted to go on foot when I go out."

8. When Confucius first heard the news of the death of his disciple, the favourite Yen Hui, he cried out in an outburst of grief, "Oh! Oh! God has forsaken me! God has forsaken me!

9. When his disciple, the favourite Yen Hui, died, Confucius burst into a paroxysm of grief. Those around him said, "Sir, you are grieving too exceedingly."

"Am I?" he replied, "But if I do not grieve exceedingly for him, for whom then should I grieve exceedingly?"

10. When the favourite, Yen Hui, died, Confucius' other disciples proposed to give him a great funeral. But Confucius said, "Do not do so for my sake."

The disciples nevertheless gave him a grand funeral.

Confucius then said to his disciples: "Hui (the favourite disciple's familiar name) behaved to me as to a father, but I have not been able to treat him as a son. It is not my fault. Ah! gentlemen, it is your fault."

11. A disciple (the intrepid ChungYu) enquired how one should behave towards the spirits of dead men.

Confucius answered, "We cannot as yet do our duties to living men; why should we enquire about our duties to dead men?"

The disciple went on to enquire about death. Confucius answered, " We do not as yet know about life ; why should we enquire about death ? "

12. On one occasion several of his disciples were standing in attendance on Confucius. One was calm and self-possessed. The intrepid Chung Yu stood upright and soldier-like. Two others looked frank and engaging. Confucius, looking on them, was pleased. He remarked, however, "There is Yu (Chung Yu's name) there,—I am afraid he will not die a natural death." [a]

13. A party in Confucius' native State proposed to build a new State-house. A disciple of Confucius remarked, " Why not keep the old building and modify it to suit the present circumstances ? Why construct a new building ? "

"That man," said Confucius, referring to the disciple, "seldom speaks ; but when he does speak, he always hits the mark."

14. Confucius on one occasion speaking in rebuke of his disciple, the intrepid Chung Yu, said : "That man with his trumpet-blowing should not be permitted to come to my house."

[a] The prophecy eventually came true. The intrepid, chivalrous Chung Yu afterwards, in defending a town against the mob in a riot, was killed. Before he expired, when his helmet had been knocked to one side in the fight, he calmly straightened it, saying : " A gentleman must die with his personal attire in proper order."

After that the other disciples began to look down upon Chung Yu. But Confucius said, "That man, in his education, has entered the gate, but not the house."

15. A disciple of Confucius, referring to two other disciples, enquired which of the two was the better man. Confucius answered, "One goes beyond the mark: the other does not come up to it." "Then," replied the disciple, "the first man is a better than the last."

"No," answered Confucius, "to go beyond the mark is just as bad as not to come up to it."

16. The head of a powerful family of nobles in Confucius' native State had amassed immense wealth. A disciple of Confucius, who was in that nobleman's service, was very exacting in collecting imposts for him from the people on his estate, thus increasing his master's already great wealth. "He is no disciple of mine," exclaimed Confucius, referring to the disciple mentioned above, and speaking to his other disciples, "Proclaim it aloud, my children, and assail him !"

17. Confucius, speaking of his four disciples, remarked, "One was simple; another was dull; another was specious; and the last was coarse."

18. Confucius, speaking of his disciple, the favourite Yen Hui, and of another disciple, remarked, "There is Hui,—(Yen Hui's name)—he is almost perfect as a man; yet he is often reduced to want. The other man does not even believe in religion; yet his possessions go on increasing. Nevertheless, the latter is often right in his judgment of things."

19. A disciple of Confucius enquired what constituted an honest man.

"An honest man," answered Confucius, "does not cant" neither does he profess esoterism," *i.e.* the secret of any -ism.

20. Confucius then went on to say, "Men now are earnest in what they profess. Are they really good and wise men? or are they serious only in appearance? That is what I should like to know."

21. A disciple, the intrepid Chung Yu, asked if he might at once carry out into practice any truth which he had learnt.

"No," answered Confucius, "You have the wishes óf your parents and of your old people at home to consult. How can you take upon yourself to carry at once into practice what you have learnt."

" Literally "does not go upon the beaten tracks," or what Carlyle calls *formulæ.*

13

Another disciple on another occasion asked the same question.

"Yes," replied Confucius, "carry it out at once."

Afterwards another disciple ventured to enquire of Confucius why he gave two totally different answers to the same question.

"That is because," answered Confucius, "the one man is too diffident ; I therefore said that to encourage him : the other man, however, is too froward; therefore I said that to pull him back."

22. When on an occasion Confucius and his disciples on their travels were threatened with danger from the violent men of a certain place, his disciple, the favourite Yen Hui, was separated from the party. Afterwards, when the disciple rejoined him, Confucius said, "I was afraid you had been killed." "While you live," answered the disciple, "how should I dare to allow myself to be killed?"

23. A member of a family of nobles who were in power in Confucius' native State, referring to two disciples of his who were in the service of that powerful· family, enquired whether those two disciples could be considered statesmen. "Oh !" replied Confucius, "I thought you had something extraordinary to ask my opinion about. You wish to have my opinion on these

men : is that all you want ?   Men I call statesmen are
those who will serve their master according to their
sense of duty ; who, however, when they find they cannot
do that, consistently with their sense of duty, will
resign.   As to those two men you refer to,—they may
be considered as states-functionaries, not statesmen."

"But," the noble went on to ask, "will these two
men carry out anything they are called upon to do?"
"An act of parricide or regicide they will not carry
out," answered Confucius.

24. A disciple of Confucius, the intrepid Chung Yu,
on one occasion got a very young man appointed Chief
Magistrate of an important town.   "You are ruining a
good man's son," said Confucius to him.

"Why," answered the disciple, "he has the large
population to deal with ; he has questions of the
interests of the country to decide upon.   Why must
one read books in order to educate himself?"

"That," replied Confucius, "is the reason why I
hate men who are always ready with an argument."

25. On one occasion five of his disciples were
sitting in attendance on Confucius.

Confucius then said to them, "I am only a little
older than you, gentlemen.   Do not mind that.   Now
living a private life, you all say that you are not known

and appreciated by men in authority ; but suppose you were known, tell me now, each of you, what would you be able to do ? "

" I could," answered the intrepid Chung Yu at once, without hesitation, " if I had the conduct of affairs in a State of even the first power which was hemmed in between two States of great power and which was embroiled in the midst of a war, and hence harassed by famine and distress—I could, if I had the conduct of affairs in such a State for three years, make the people brave and, moreover, know their duty."

On hearing this, Confucius only smiled ; and, turning to another disciple, said : " And you—what do you say ? "

" I could," answered the disciple appealed to, " If I had the conduct of the government of a State, say, of the third or fourth power, I could in such a case, after three years, make the people live in plenty.   As to education in higher things, I would leave that to the good and wise men who will come after me."

Confucius then turned to another disciple and said : " Now you—what do you say ? "

" I do not say," replied the disciple, " that in what I am going to suppose I *could do* what I propose ; only, I would *try* to do it.   Suppose then there were

functions to be performed in any Court, such as public
receptions and general assemblies,—dressed in an appropriate uniform, I think I could be the vice-presiding officer."

"And now you," said Confucius to the last of the
four disciples, "what do you say?"

The disciple thus last appealed to, then laid aside
the harpsichord which he was thrumming, stood up
and answered: "What I have in my mind differs
entirely from what those three gentlemen have
proposed."

"What harm is there in that?" replied Confucius,—
"we are all only speaking out each his own mind."
"Then," answered the disciple, "we will suppose now
that we are in the latter days of spring, when we have
changed all our winter clothing for fresh, new, light gar-
ments for the warmer weather.   I would then propose
that we take along with us five or six grown-up young
friends and six or seven still younger men.   We will
then bathe in that romantic river; after which we will
go to the top of that ancient terrace to air and cool
ourselves; and at last we will return, singing on our
way as we loiter back to our homes."

"Ah!" said Confucius then, with a sigh, "I agree
with him."

Afterwards, when three of the above four disciples had left, the one who spoke the last word and who remained behind, enquired of Confucius, saying: "What do you think of what those three gentlemen said?"

"They, of course," answered Confucius, "only spoke out, each his own mind."

"But," asked the disciple, "why did you smile at the first speaker?"

"Oh," replied Confucius, "To rule a country requires judgment and modesty. But what the first speaker said was not modest,—therefore I smiled at him."

"But the second speaker," the disciple went on to ask, "Did he not speak of the affairs of a nation?" "Why," answered Confucius, "Did you ever hear of a State of even the third or fourth power that is not a nation?" "Well then," the disciple went on further to ask,—"the third speaker,—did he not also mean the affairs of a great nation in what he said?"

"Where there are courts, public receptions, general assemblies," answered Confucius,—"Where do you find such things except in the Courts of the princes of the Empire. The third speaker modestly said he would be a vice-presiding officer at such functions. If such a man as he is fit only to be a vice-president who would be fit to be the president?"

CHAPTER XII.

1. A disciple of Confucius, the favourite Yen Hui, enquired what constituted a moral life. Confucius answered, "Renounce yourself and conform to the ideal of decency and good sense. [68]

"If one could only," Confucius went on to say, "live a moral life, renouncing himself and conforming to the ideal of decency and good sense for one single day, the world would become moral. To be moral, a man depends entirely upon himself and not upon others."

The disciple then asked for practical rules to be observed in living a moral life.

Confucius answered, "Whatsoever things are contrary to the ideal of decency and good sense, do not look upon them. Whatsoever things are contrary to the ideal of decency and good sense, do not listen to

[68] D'ALEMBERT remarked that the ancient Stoic Diogenes would be the greatest man in antiquity in Europe, if he only had "decency."

The first part is the self-renunciation (Entsagen) of GOETHE :

"Stirb und werde
Denn so lang du das nicht hast,
Bist du nur ein trüber Gast
Auf der dunklen Erde."

The second part is the imperious ideal of Art (禮)—of the Greeks and Italians, which in itself, as GOETHE says, *is* religion.

them. Whatsoever things are contrary to the ideal of decency and good sense, do not utter them with your mouth. Lastly, let nothing in whatsoever things you do, act or move, be contrary to the ideal of decency and good sense."

2. Another disciple of Confucius on another occasion asked what constituted a moral life.

Confucius answered, "When going out into the world, behave always as if you were at an audience before the Emperor; in dealing with the people, act as if you were at worship before God. Whatsoever things you do not wish that others should do unto you, do not do unto them. In your public life in the State as well as in your private life in your family, give no one a just cause of complaint against you."

The disciple then said: "Unworthy and remiss though I am, I shall try to make what you have just said the rule of my life."

3. Another disciple asked what constituted a moral character.

Confucius answered, "A man of moral character is one who is sparing of his words."

"To be sparing of words : does that alone," asked the disciple, "constitute a moral character ?"

"Why," replied Confucius, "When a man feels the difficulty of *living* a moral life, would he be otherwise than sparing of his words?"

4. The same disciple asked what constituted a good and wise man.

Confucius answered, "A good and wise man is without anxiety and without fear." "To be without anxiety and without fear : does that alone," asked the disciple, "constitute a good and wise man?"

"Why," replied Confucius, "When a man finds within himself no cause for self-reproach, what has he to be anxious about ; what has he to fear?"

5. A disciple of Confucius was unhappy, exclaiming often : "All men have their brothers : I alone have none." Upon which another disciple said to him, "I have heard it said that Life and Death are pre-ordained, and riches and honours come from God. A good and wise man is serious and without blame. In his conduct towards others he behaves with earnestness, and with judgment and good sense. In that way he will find all men within the corners of the Earth his brothers. What reason, then, has a good and wise man to complain that he has no brothers in his home?"

6. A disciple of Confucius enquired what constituted perspicuity.

14

Confucius answered, "A man who can resist long-continued attempts of others to insinuate prejudice into him, or one who cannot be influenced by a sudden appeal to his own personal safety :—such a man may be considered a man of perspicuity.   Indeed, a man who can resist such an influence, or such an appeal, must be a really superior man."

7. A disciple on one occasion enquired what was essential in the government of a country.

Confucius answered, "There must be sufficient food for the people ; an efficient army ; and confidence of the people in their rulers."

"But," asked the disciple then, "If one were compelled to dispense with one of those three things, which one of them should go first ? "

"Dispense with the army," replied Confucius.

"But still," the disciple went on to ask, "If one were compelled to dispense with one of those two things remaining, which one of them should go first ? "

"Dispense with the food," replied Confucius, "For from of old men have died, but without the confidence of the people in their rulers, there can be no government."

8. An officer of a certain State on one occasion remarked to a disciple of Confucius, saying : "A wise

and good man wants only the substance ; why should he trouble about the style ?"

"I am sorry to hear you make such a statement," replied Confucius' disciple, "What you would say is true ; but, stated in that way, it is impossible for men not to misunderstand your meaning. To be sure, the style comes out of the substance, but the substance also comes out of the style. For the substance in the skin of a tiger or a leopard is the same as the substance in the skin of a dog or a sheep."[59]

9. The reigning prince of Confucius' native State on one occasion asked one of Confucius' disciples, saying : "The year now is one of scarcity : we cannot make the revenue meet the public expenditure. What should be done?"

The disciple answered, "Why not tithe (take one-tenth) the people ?" "Why," replied the prince, "with two-thirds, even, we cannot make ends meet : how should we be able to do so with only one-tenth ?" To which the disciple answered, "When the people have plenty, the prince will not want. But if the people want, the prince will not have plenty."

10. A disciple of Confucius enquired how to raise the moral sentiment and to dispel delusions in life.

---

[59] Speaking of style in literature, WORDSWORTH says, "To be sure, it was the *manner*, but then, you know, the matter always comes out of the manner."— EMERSON'S "*English Traits.*"

Confucius answered, "Make conscientiousness and sincerity your first principles. Act up to what is right. In that way you will raise the moral sentiment in you.

"You wish to live and hate to die. But while clinging to life, you yet hanker after those things which can only shorten life : that is a great delusion in life.

> Truly your wealth and pelf avail you nought,
> To have what others want, is all you sought.*

11. The reigning prince of a certain State asked Confucius what was essential in the government of a country.

Confucius answered, "Let the prince *be* a prince, and the public servant *be* a public servant. Let the father *be* a father, and let the son *be* a son."

"It is very true," replied the prince, "Indeed, if the prince *is* not a prince, and the public servant *is* not a public servant, and if the father *is* not a father and the son *is* not a son,—in such a state of things, even though I had my revenue, how should I enjoy it ?"

12. Confucius, speaking of his disciple, the intrepid Chung Yu, remarked : "One who can settle a dispute with half a sentence—that is Yu" (Chung Yu's name).

It was also remarked of the same disciple that he never slept a night over a promise.

---

* A Chinese Commentator believes that the verse should be transferred to Chapter XVI, Section 12.

13. Confucius on one occasion after he had been appointed Chief Justice in his native State, remarked : "While sitting in court, in deciding upon the suits that come before me, I am no better than other men. But what I always try to do is to make even the suits unnecessary."

14. A disciple of Confucius enquired what was the essential thing in the conduct of the government of a country.

Confucius answered, "Be patient in maturing your plans and then carry them out with conscientiousness."

15. Confucius remarked, "A man who studies extensively the arts and literature, and directs his studies with judgment and taste, is not likely to get into a wrong track." [61]

16. Confucius remarked, "A good and wise man encourages men to develop the good qualities in their nature, and not their bad qualities ; whereas, a bad man and a fool does the very opposite."

17. A noble who was the minister in power in Confucius' native State asked him to define government.

"Government means order," answered Confucius. "If you yourself, sir, are in order, who will dare to be disorderly ? "

[61] Repetition of Chapter VI, Section 5,

18. The noble mentioned above was distressed at the frequency of robberies in the country. He asked Confucius what should be done.

"If you yourself," answered Confucius, "show them that you do not wish for wealth, although you should reward them for stealing, the people would not steal."

19. The same noble again asked about government, saying, "What do you say to putting to death the wicked in the interests of the good?"

"In your government," answered Confucius, "why should you think it necessary to depend upon capital punishments? Wish for honesty, and the people will be honest. The moral power of the rulers is as the wind, and that of the people is as the grass. Whithersoever the wind blows, the grass is sure to bend."

20. A disciple of Confucius enquired, "What must an educated gentleman do in order to be distinguished?"

"What do you mean by being distinguished?" asked Confucius.

"I mean," replied the disciple, "that whether in public life or in private life he will be heard of by the world."

"That," answered Confucius, "is to be notorious, not distinguished.

"Now a man who is really a man of distinction is one who stands upon his own integrity and loves what is right : who forms a correct judgment of men by observing how they look as well as by regarding what they say. Reflection makes him humble in his estimate of himself as compared with other men. Such a man, whether he be in public life or in private life, will be a distinguished man.

"As to the notorious man : he is one who wants to be moral in his look and outward appearance, but really is not so in his life. He prides himself on such an appearance without misgiving. Such a man in public life or in private life, will also certainly be heard of and known."

21. A disciple of Confucius on one occasion was in Confucius' company when he went out for a walk on a terrace built for a religious purpose. The disciple then took the occasion to ask him what one should do in order to elevate the moral sentiment ; to discover the secret vices and failings in one's inmost mind ; and, lastly, to dispel the delusions of life."

"That is a very good question indeed," answered Confucius.

"Make it a rule," he then said, "to *work* for it before you accept anything as your own : that is, perhaps, the best way to elevate the moral sentiment.

"Make it a habit to assail your own vices and failings before you assail the vices and failings of others: that is, perhaps, the best way to discover the secret vices of your inmost mind.

"If a man allows himself to lose his temper and forget himself of a morning, in such a way as to become careless for the safety of his own person and for the safety of his parents and friends:—is that not a case of a great delusion in life?"

22. The same disciple mentioned above asked, "What does a moral life consist in?"

"The moral life of a man," answered Confucius, "consists in loving men."*

The disciple then asked, "What does understanding consist in?"

"Understanding," answered Confucius, "consists in understanding men."

The disciple, however, did not seem to comprehend the meaning of what was said. Thereupon Confucius

---

* The Chinese word 仁, which we have all along translated "moral life and moral character" means literally "humanity."

"The aim in education," says COMENIUS, "is to train generally all who are born men to all what is *human*."

went on to say, " Uphold the cause of the just, and put down every cause that is unjust in such a way that the unjust will be made just."

When the disciple left, he met on the way another disciple, and said to him : " Just a little while ago I saw the Master, and enquired of him what understanding consisted in, and he answered, ' Uphold the cause of the just, and put down every cause that is unjust in such a way that the unjust will be made just. What did he mean by that ?"

" It is a saying," replied the other disciple, "very wide indeed in its application. When the ancient Emperor Shun came to the government of the Empire and, selecting from among the people, advanced Kao Yao to be Minister of Justice : from that moment all immoral people disappeared. When the ancient Emperor the great T'ang came to the government of the Empire and, choosing from among the people, advanced I-yin to be Prime Minister : from that moment, all immoral men disappeared."

23. A disciple of Confucius enquired how one should behave to a friend.

Confucius answered, " Be conscientious in what you say to him ! Lead him on gently to what you would

15

have him be ; if you find you cannot do that, stop. Do not quarrel with him only to get insulted."

24. A disciple of Confucius remarked, " A wise man makes friends by his taste for art and literature. He uses his friends to help him to live a moral life."

CHAPTER XIII.

1. A disciple of Confucius enquired how to conduct the government of a country.

Confucius answered, "Go before the people with your example ; show them your exertion." The disciple asked for something more. "Be indefatigable in that," replied Confucius.

2. Another disciple, who was in the service of a powerful noble in Confucius' native State, enquired how to conduct the government of the country.

Confucius answered, "Leave the initiative in the details of government to the responsible heads of the departments. Overlook small short-comings ; and advance men of ability and worth."

"But," answered the disciple, "how am I to know who are men of ability and worth?"

"Advance those," replied Confucius, "whom you already know : there is then no fear that those whom you do not know will be neglected."

3. A disciple, the intrepid Chung Yu, said to Confucius on one occasion when the reigning prince of a certain State was negotiating for Confucius to enter

his service : "The prince is waiting, sir, to entrust the government of the country to you. Now what do you consider the first thing to be done ?"

"If I must begin," answered Confucius, "I would begin by defining the names of things."

"Oh ! really," replied the disciple,—"but you are too impractical. What has definition of names to do here ?"

"Sir," replied Confucius, "you have really no manners. A gentleman, when he hears anything he does not understand, will always wait for an explanation.

" Now, if names of things are not properly defined, *words* will not correspond to *facts*. When words do not correspond to facts, it is impossible to perfect anything. Where it is impossible to perfect anything, the arts and institutions of civilisation cannot flourish. When the arts and institutions of civilisation cannot flourish, law and justice cannot attain their ends ; and when law and justice do not attain their ends, the people will be at a loss to know what to do.

" Therefore a wise and good man can always specify whatever he names ; whatever he can specify, he can carry out. A wise and good man makes it a point always to be exact[a] in the words he uses."

4. A disciple of Confucius requested to be taught farming. Confucius answered, "For that I am not as good as an old farmer."

The disciple then asked to be taught gardening. "For that," replied Confucius, "I am not as good as an old gardener."

After the disciple had left, Confucius remarked, "What a petty-minded man he is!"

"When the rulers of a country," he then went on to say, "encourage education and good manners the people will never fail in respect! When the rulers encourage the love of justice, the people will never fail in obedience; when the rulers encourage good faith, the people will never fail in honesty. In such case, people from all quarters will flock to that country :—what need then has a ruler to know about husbandry?"

[a] Literally "not careless." CONFUCIUS here points out, as a characteristic of his time, what the Revd. Mr. SMITH in his *Chinese Characteristics* has lately very cleverly pointed out as a characteristic of the Chinese of the present day, namely "a want of exactness," which, wherever and whenever it exists makes it impossible for the arts of civilisation to flourish. But "the want of exactness" in the use of words, we fancy, is not entirely confined to China now. *See* note Chapter VI, Section 28.

5. Confucius remarked, "A man who can recite three hundred pieces of poetry by heart, but who, when the conduct of the affairs of a nation is entrusted to him, can do nothing, and who, when sent on a public mission to a foreign country, has nothing to say for himself,—although such a man has much learning, of what use is it ?"

6. Confucius remarked, "If a man is in order in his personal conduct, he will get served even without taking the trouble to give orders. But if a man is not in order in his personal conduct, he may give orders, but his orders will not be obeyed."

7. Confucius remarked of the state of government of his own State and that of another State in his time: "The one is about the same as the other."

8. Confucius remarked of a public character of the time that he was admirable in the way in which he ordered the economy of his home. Confucius said: "When he had saved something from his income, he would remark, 'I have just made ends meet.' Later on, when he had increased his saving, he would remark, 'I have just managed to pay for all I require.' Finally, when he had saved a large surplus, he would remark, 'Now I can just manage to get along pretty well.'"

9. When Confucius on his travels was on one occasion entering a certain State in company with a disciple who was driving the carriage for him, he remarked, "What a large population is here!"

"With such a large population," asked the disciple, "what should be done?" "Enrich them," answered Confucius. "And after that?" asked the disciple. "Educate them," replied Confucius.

10. Confucius on one occasion remarked, "If I were given the conduct of the government of a country now, in one year I should have accomplished something; after three years, I should have put everything in order."

11. Confucius went on to remark, "It is a common saying that if good honest men had the rule of a country for a hundred years, they could make deeds of violence impossible and could thus dispense with capital punishment. It is a very true saying!"

12. Confucius finally remarked, "If a really God-sent great man were to become Emperor now, it would still take a generation before the people could be moral."

13. Confucius remarked, "If a man has really put his personal conduct in order, what is there in the government of a country that he should find any

difficulty in it? But if a man has not put his personal conduct in order, how can he put in order the people of a country?"

14. On one occasion when a disciple who was in official employment returned from the palace, Confucius said to him, "Why are you so late?" "Oh!" answered the disciple, "We have just had State affairs." "You mean 'business'! For if there had been State affairs, although I am not now in office, I should still have been consulted."⁶⁴

15. The reigning prince of Confucius' native State enquired if the principle to make a country prosperous could be expressed in one single sentence. Confucius answered, "One cannot expect so much meaning from a single sentence. There is, however, a saying which the people have, 'To be a ruler of men is difficult and to be a public servant is not easy.' Now if one only knew that it is difficult to be a ruler of men, would not that alone almost make a country prosperous?"

The prince then asked if the principle to ruin a country could be expressed in one single sentence.

Confucius answered, "So much meaning is not to be expected from one single sentence. There is, however, a saying among the people: 'I find no

⁶⁴ Confucius was then a member of the State council.

pleasure in being a ruler of men, except in that what-soever I order no man shall oppose.' Now if what is ordered is right, it is well and good that no one oppose it; but if what is ordered is not right and no one opposes it,—is not that alone enough to ruin a country?"

16. The prince of a small principality asked what was essential in the government of a country.

Confucius answered, "When there is good government in a country the people at home are happy, and the people in other countries will come."

17. A disciple of Confucius who was appointed chief magistrate of an important town enquired what was essential in government.

Confucius answered, "Do not be in a hurry to get things done. Do not consider petty advantages. If you are in a hurry to get things done, things will not be done thoroughly and well. If you consider petty advantages, you will never accomplish great things."

18. The reigning prince of a small principality said to Confucius, "Among my people there are men to be found who are so upright that when a father steals a sheep the son is ready to bear witness against him."

"In our country," replied Confucius, "The upright men are different from that. They consider it consistent

16

with true uprightness for a father to be silent regarding the misdeed of his son and for a son to be silent concerning the misdeed of his father."

19. A disciple of Confucius enquired what was essential in a moral life. Confucius answered, " In dealing with yourself, be serious ; in business, be earnest ; in intercourse with other men, be conscientious. Although you may be living among barbarians and savages, these principles cannot be neglected."

20. A disciple of Confucius enquired, "What must one be in order to be considered a gentleman?" Confucius answered,"He must be a man of strict personal honour ; when sent on a public mission to any country, he will not disgrace his mission. Such a man may be considered a gentleman."

The disciple then asked for a type of gentleman next in degree to the one mentioned above. Confucius answered, " One whom the members of his family hold up as a good son and his fellow citizens hold up as a good citizen."

The disciple went on to ask for a type of gentleman still next in degree.

Confucius answered, " One who makes it a point to carry out what he says and to persist in what he undertakes, a dogged, stubborn little gentleman though he is ; such a man may also be considered a type of gentleman next in degree."

The disciple finally asked, saying, " But now what is your opinion of the gentlemen now in the public service?" "They are," replied Confucius, "only red-taped[65] bureaucrats not worth taking into account."

21. Confucius remarked, "If I cannot find equitable and reasonable men to have to do with, upon necessity I would choose men of enthusiastic or even fanatical[66] character. Enthusiastic men are zealous and there are always limits which fanatical men would not pass."

22. Confucius remarked, "The southern people have a saying, ' A man without perseverance cannot be a doctor or a magician.' How true !

"Again, it is said in the *I-king*, ' The reputation for a virtue once acquired unless persevered in will lead to disgrace.' "

Commenting on this, Confucius remarked, "It is much better not to assume the reputation for the virtue at all."[67]

---

[65] The Chinese expression for " red tape " is " pecks and hampers," from the fact that the duty of mere routine officers in ancient times was to weigh and measure the grain and other produce collected from the people."

[66] Literally dog-ged—the Chinese character meaning a fierce, tenacious animal like the bull-dog. In fact, man with a fixed idea.

[67] The great Chinese commentator, Chu Fu-tzu gives up this last passage, saying that he does not understand it. We venture here to submit the above explanation of the passage as given in the translation.

23. Confucius remarked, "A wise man is sociable, but not familiar. A fool is familiar but not sociable."

24. A disciple of Confucius enquired of him, saying, "What do you say of a man who is popular with all his fellow townsmen in a place?"

"He is not necessarily a good man," answered Confucius.

"What do you say then," asked the disciple, "of a man who is unpopular with all his fellow townsmen?"

"He is neither," replied Confucius, "necessarily a good nor a bad man. A really good man is he who is popular with the good men of a place and unpopular with the bad men."

25. Confucius remarked, "A wise and good man is easy to serve, but difficult to please. If you go beyond your duty to please him, he will not be pleased. But in his employment of men, he always takes into consideration their capacity. A fool, on the other hand, is easy to please, but difficult to serve. If you go beyond your duty to please him, he will be pleased. But in his employment of men, he expects them to be able to do everything."

26. Confucius remarked, "A wise man is dignified, but not proud. A fool is proud, but not dignified."

27. Confucius remarked, "A man of strong, resolute, simple character approaches nearly to the true moral character."

28. A disciple of Confucius enquired, "What must a man be in order to be considered a gentleman?" Confucius answered, "He must be sympathetic, obliging and affectionate: sympathetic and obliging to his friends and affectionate to the members of his family."

29. Confucius remarked, "A good honest man, after educating the people for seven years, will be able to lead them to war."

30. Confucius remarked, "To allow a people to go to battle without first instructing them, is to betray them."

CHAPTER XIV.

1. A disciple of Confucius enquired what constituted dishonour. Confucius answered, "When there
is justice and order in the government of the country, to
think only of pay is dishonourable. When there is no
justice and order in the government of the country, to
think only of pay is also dishonourable."

2. The same disciple went on to ask, saying: "A
man with whom ambition, vanity, envy and selfishness
have ceased to act as motives,—may he be considered
a moral character?" "What you suggest," answered
Confucius, "may be considered as something difficult
to achieve; but I cannot say that it constitutes a moral
character."

3. Confucius remarked, "A gentleman who only
thinks of the comforts of life, cannot be a true
gentleman."

4. Confucius remarked, "When there is justice
and order in the government of the country a man may
be bold and lofty in the expression of his opinions as
well as in his actions. When, however, there is no
justice and order in the government of the country, a

man may be bold and lofty in his action, but he should be reserved in the expression of his opinions."

5. Confucius remarked, "A man who possesses moral worth will always have something to say worth listening to ; but a man who has something to say is not necessarily a man of moral worth. A moral character always has courage ; but a man of courage is not necessarily a moral character.

6. A disciple of Confucius on one occasion remarked in his presence : "There was a famous man in ancient time who was an excellent marksman in archery, and there was another man famous for his feats of strength : both of these men eventually came to an unnatural end. On the other hand, there were also in ancient time two men who worked in the fields and toiled as husbandmen : both these latter finally came to the government of the Empire."

Confucius at the time did not say anything in reply. But when the disciple had left, Confucius said : "What a really wise and good man he is ! How much he honours moral worth in what he has said !"

7. Confucius remarked, " There are wise men who are not moral characters ; but a fool is never a moral character."

8. Confucius remarked, "Where there is affection, exertion is made easy; where there is disinterestedness, instruction will not be neglected."

9. Confucius, speaking of the great merits of the State documents of a certain State of the time, remarked : "In the preparation of these State documents, one minister would first sketch out the draft ; another would then discuss the several points ; another minister after that would make the necessary corrections ; and finally, another minister would polish the style and give it a last finishing touch."

10. Someone on one occasion asked Confucius' opinion of the character of a famous statesman (the Colbert of the time). Confucius answered, "He was a generous man."

The enquirer asked of the character of another notorious statesman. "Why, that man! That man! Why speak of him at all ?"

The enquirer finally asked of the character of Kuan Chung (the Bismarck of the time). Confucius answered, "As a man he was able to take possession of an estate, confiscated from the head of an old noble family in the country, in such a way that the former owner, although he was thus obliged to live in great poverty to the end of his days, yet had nothing to say in complaint against Kuan Chung."

11. Confucius remarked, "To be poor without complaining is not easy; but it is easy to be rich without being proud."

12. Confucius remarked of a public character of the time: "As an officer in the retinue of a great noble, he would be excellent, but he is not fit to be councillor of State even in a small principality."

13. A disciple of Confucius enquired what constituted a perfect character. Confucius, referring to the different famous known men of the time, said: "A perfect character should have the intellect of such a man; the disinterestedness of such another man; the gallantry of such another; the accomplishments of such another man. In addition to those qualities, if he would culture himself by the study of the arts and institutions of the civilised world, he would then be considered a perfect character."

"But," Confucius went on to say, "now-a-days it is not even necessary to be all that in order to be a perfect character. One who, when he sees a personal advantage, can think of what is right and, in presence of personal danger, is ready to give up his life; and who, under long-continued trying circumstances, does not belie

17

the professions of his life :—such a man may also be considered a perfect character."

14. Confucius on one occasion enquired about a teacher from one of his disciples, saying : " Is it true that your teacher seldom speaks and seldom laughs ; and that he never accepts anything from anybody ? " " They are mistaken who say that," replied the teacher's disciple, "My teacher speaks when it is time to speak : therefore people never lose patience when he does speak. He laughs when he is really delighted ; therefore people never lose patience when he does laugh. He accepts when it is consistent with right to accept : therefore people never lose patience when he accepts anything." Confucius then said, "So ! is it really so with him."

15. Confucius, speaking of a powerful noble of his native State, remarked, " He took possession of an important military town when sending a message to the prince to beg him to appoint a successor to his own family estate. Although it is said that on that occasion he did not use intimidation with the prince, his master, I do not believe it."

16. Confucius, speaking of the characters of the two most famous princes of his time, remarked : " One (the Frederic the Great of the time) was crafty and without

honour. The other (Wilhelm I of Germany) was a man of honour and without any craftiness in his character."

17. A disciple, speaking of the famous statesman Kuan Chung (the Bismarck of the time), remarked, "Kuan Chung and another officer were given charge, as tutors, of the elder of two princes. When the younger of the two princes, in order to succeed to the throne, slew his elder brother, the other officer preferred to die with his pupil and charge, but Kuan Chung did not die. Did not Kuan Chung in this show that he was not a moral character ?"

Confucius answered, "It was due to the great services of Kuan Chung that the prince, his master, was able to call together the princes of the Empire to a Congress which prevented a general war during the time. What has one to say against the moral character— what has one to say against the moral character of a man like that ?" [68]

18. Another disciple then remarked, "But Kuan Chung not only did not die with the elder prince, his pupil and charge ; he even served the younger prince, the very man who murdered his pupil and charge.

* The Berlin Congress of the time. *See* note, Chapter III, Section 22.

Did he not in this show that he was not a moral character?"

Confucius answered, "Kuan Chung as Prime Minister enabled the prince, his master, to exercise Imperialism over the princes of the time, to unite the Empire and give it peace. Down to the present day the people are enjoying the benefits due to his great services. But for Kuan Chung we should now be living like savages. He was certainly not like your faithful lover and his sweetheart among the common people, who, in order to prove their constancy, go and drown themselves in a ditch, nobody taking any notice of them."

19. A noble of a certain State (who after his death was given the title of Beauclerc), when he was called to office in the government, chose for his colleague an officer who had been serving in his retinue. Confucius, remarking on this, said: "Such a man certainly deserves the title of 'Beauclerc.'"

20. Confucius on one occasion was commenting on the scandalous life of the prince [49] of a certain State, when somebody remarked, "If he was such a man—

* The Charles II of the time :
"A merry monarch, scandalous and poor."
His wife is the notorious princess mentioned in Chapter VI, Section 26.

how did he not lose his throne ?" "That was because," replied Confucius, "he had great and able men to carry on the different departments of his administration."

21. Confucius remarked, " From a man who is not bashful in his talk, it is difficult to expect much in the way of action."

22. On one occasion, having heard that the Prime Minister of a neighbouring State had murdered the prince, his master, Confucius, after purifying himself as when going to worship, presented himself before the prince of his own State, and said : "The minister of the neighbouring State has murdered the Prince, his master. I beg that steps to bring him to a summary punishment may be at once undertaken." But the prince only answered : "Go and tell our ministers in the government."

Confucius then went out, saying as he went : " As I have the honour to sit in the State council of the country, I have thought it my duty to bring this to the notice of my prince ; but he, my prince, now tells me to go and inform the ministers." Confucius accordingly went to see the ministers then in power, and told them what he had said to the prince ; but the ministers also would not do anything in the matter. Confucius then said : "As I have the honour to be a member of the State council of the country, I have done my duty in bringing this to your notice."

23. A disciple of Confucius enquired how one should behave towards the prince, his master. Confucius answered, "Do not impose upon him and, if necessary, withstand him to his face."

24. Confucius remarked, "A wise and good man looks upwards in his aspirations; a fool looks downwards."

25. Confucius remarked, "Men in old times educated themselves for their own sakes. Men now educate themselves to impress others."

26. An officer of a certain State, who was an old friend of Confucius, sent a messenger with a message of enquiry to him. Confucius, after making the messenger sit down with him, said to him; "What has your master been doing?" "My master," replied the messenger, "has been trying to reduce the number of his shortcomings without, however, being able to do so."

When the messenger had left, Confucius exclaimed "What a messenger! What a messenger!"

27. Confucius remarked, "A man who is not in office in the government of a country should not give advice as to its policy." [70]

---

[70] Repetition of Chapter VII, Section 14.

28. A disciple of Confucius remarked, "A wise man should never occupy his thoughts with anything outside of his position."

29. Confucius remarked, "A wise man is ashamed to *say* much ; he prefers to *do* more."

30. Confucius once remarked, "A wise and good man may be known in three ways which I am not able to show in my own person. As a moral man he is free from anxiety ; as a man of understanding he is free from doubt ; and as a man of courage he is free from fear."

A disciple, who heard what Confucius said, then remarked, "That is only what *you* say of yourself, sir."

31. A disciple of Confucius was fond of criticising men and making comparisons. Confucius said to him, "You must be a very superior man to be able to do that. For myself, I have no time for it."

32. Confucius remarked, "Be not concerned that men do not know you ; be concerned that you have no ability."

33. Confucius remarked, "A man who does not anticipate deceit nor imagine untrustworthiness, but who can readily detect their presence, must be a very superior man."

34. A practical character of the time said once to Confucius, "What do you mean by rambling about with your talk? I am afraid you are also but a self-seeking good talker." "I do not wish," replied Confucius, "to be a good talker; but I hate narrow-minded bigotry in men."

35. Confucius remarked, "A good horse is considered so, not because of its mere brute strength, but because of its moral qualities."

36, Someone on one occasion enquired of Confucius, saying: "What do you say of requiting injury with kindness?" Confucius replied, "How will you then requite kindness? Requite injury with justice and kindness with kindness."

37. Confucius on one occasion remarked, "Ah! there is no one who understands me." Thereupon a disciple asked, "What do you mean, sir, in saying that no one understands you?" Confucius then answered, "I do not repine against God, nor do I complain of men. My studies are among lowly things, but my thoughts penetrate the sublime. Ah! There is perhaps only God who understands me."

38. A man having on one occasion slandered Confucius and his disciple, the intrepid Chung Yu, to a noble of the Court, somebody informed Chung Yu of it.

Chung Yu afterwards, in speaking of it to Confucius, said, "My Lord———is being led astray by that man ; but I am strong enough to exterminate that man and expose his carcase on the market-place." Upon which Confucius said, "Whether or not I shall succeed in carrying out my teaching among men, depends upon the will of God. What can that man do against the will of God."

39. Confucius remarked on one occasion : "Men of real moral worth now retire from the world altogether. Some of less degree of worth avoid or retire from certain countries. Some of still less degree of worth retire as soon as they are looked upon with disfavour. Some of the least degree of worth retire when they are told to do so."

40. Confucius went on to say, "I know of seven men who have written books." [71]

41. A disciple of Confucius, the intrepid Chung Yu, had on one occasion to pass a night before the gate of a city. The keeper of the gate, on seeing him, asked, "Where are you from, sir ?" "I am from Confucius," replied Chung Yu. "Oh," said the other, "isn't it he

---

[71] We here venture to translate the word 作 as "to write books and propound theories." The great Chinese Commentator gives up this passage, saying that he does not understand the reference.

18

who knows the impracticalness of the times, and is yet trying to do something ? " [73]

42. Confucius was on one occasion playing upon a musical instrument when a man carrying a basket passed the door of the house. " Ah ! " said the man on hearing the sound of the music, " He has his heart full, the musician who is playing there ! " After a while, he said, " How contemptible to go on thrumming like that when nobody takes any notice of you : you should stop !

> " You must swim over when the water is high,
> But in low water you may ' paidle ' [73] and keep dry."

On hearing what the man said, Confucius remarked : " That certainly shows determination ; but it is not difficult." [74]

43. A disciple of Confucius enquired of him, saying, " What is meant when the Book of Records says that an ancient Emperor while observing the period of Imperial mourning, kept silence for three years ? "

Confucius answered, " That was the rule not only in the case of that particular Emperor : it was a general

---

[73] Men of real worth in CONFUCIUS' time all retired from the world : and in order to earn an honest livelihood took to mean employments, such as here that of a gate-keeper. In Europe, the world-famous philosopher SPINOZA took to glass-grinding !

[73] " Paidle "—Scotch for " wade,"
> " We twa hae paidl't in the burn."

[74] i.e. To leave the world in contempt and disgust,

rule with all princes of antiquity. When the sovereign died, for three years all public functionaries received their orders from the Chief Minister."

44. Confucius remarked, "When the rulers encourage education and good manners, the people are easily amenable to government."

45. A disciple of Confucius enquired what constituted a wise and good man.

Confucius answered, "A wise and good man is one who sets himself seriously to order his conversation aright?" "Is that all?" asked the disciple. "Yes," replied Confucius, "He wants to order his conversation aright for the happiness of others." "Is that all?" asked the disciple again. "Yes," replied Confucius, "He wants to order his conversation aright for the happiness of the world; and, judged by that, even the great ancient Emperors felt their shortcomings."

46. A worthless man, well known to Confucius, was on one occasion squatting on his heels, and did not rise up when Confucius passed by him. Confucius then said to him: "A wilful man and a bad citizen in your youth, in manhood you have done nothing to distinguish yourself, and now you are dishonouring your old age: such a man is called a rascal!" With that, Confucius lifted his staff and hit him on the shanks.

47. A youth of a certain place was employed by Confucius in his house to answer the door and introduce visitors. Someone remarked to Confucius, "I suppose he has improved in his education." "No," replied Confucius, "I have observed him sitting where a youth of his age should not sit, and walking side by side with people who are his seniors. He is not one who seeks to improve his education; he is only one who is in a great hurry to become a grown-up man."

CHAPTER XV.

1. The reigning prince of a certain State where Confucius was on a visit on his travels, asked about military tactics. "I know a little about the arts of peace," replied Confucius, "but I have never studied the art of war." The next day he left the country.

Then, going on in his travels, he arrived at another State. Their provisions having failed them, his party had to go without food, and were so reduced that they could not proceed. A disciple, the intrepid Chung Yu, with discontent in his look, then said to Confucius, "A wise man and good man—can he, too, be reduced to such distress?" "Yes," replied Confucius, "a wise and good man sometimes also meets with distress; but a fool, when in distress, becomes reckless."

2. Confucius once remarked to a disciple, "You think, I suppose, that I am one who has learned many things and remembers them all?" "Yes," replied the disciple, "but is it not so?"

"No," answered Confucius, "I unite all my knowledge by one connecting principle."

3. Confucius on one occasion remarked to a disciple, "It is seldom that men understand real moral worth."

4. Confucius remarked, "The ancient Emperor Shun was perhaps the one man who successfully carried out the principle of no-government. For what need is there really for what is called government? A ruler needs only to be earnest in his personal conduct, and to behave in a manner worthy of his position."[15]

5. A disciple of Confucius enquired what one should do in order to get along well with men. Confucius answered, "Be conscientious and sincere in what you say; be earnest and serious in what you do: in that way, although you might be in barbarous countries, you will get along well with men. But if, in what you say, you are not conscientious and sincere, and, in what you do, you are not earnest and serious, even in your own country and in your home, how can you get along well

[15] The American EMERSON, on a visit to Stonehenge in England in company with CARLYLE, writes: "On Sunday my friends asked whether there were any Americans with an American idea? Thus challenged, * * * I opened the dogma of *no-government* and non-resistance. * * I said: 'It is true that I have 'never seen in any country a man of sufficient valour to stand up for this truth, and 'yet it is plain to me that no less valour than this can command my respect. 'I can see the bankruptcy of the vulgar musket-worship,—though great men are 'musket worshippers; and 't is certain, as God liveth, the gun that does not need 'another gun, the law of love and justice alone, can effect a clean revolution.'"— *English Traits.*

with men? Keep these principles constantly before you, as when, driving a carriage, you keep your eyes on the head of your horse. In that way you will always get along well with men."

The disciple had these words engraved on his belt.

6. Confucius, speaking of a famous historiographer of the time, remarked, "What a straightforward man he was! When there were justice and order in the government of his country, he was straight as an arrow; when there were no justice and order, he was still straight as an arrow."

Speaking of another public character of the time, Confucius remarked, "What a really wise and good man he was! When there were justice and order in the government of his country, he entered the public service; but when there were no justice and order, he rolled himself up and led a strictly private life."

7. Confucius remarked, "When you meet the proper person to speak to and do not speak out, you lose your opportunity; but when you meet one who is not a proper person to speak to and you speak to him, you waste your words. A man of intelligence never loses his opportunity, neither does he waste his words."

8. Confucius remarked, "A gentleman of spirit or a man of moral character will never try to save his life

at the expense of his moral character : he prefers to
sacrifice his life in order to save his moral character."

9. A disciple of Confucius enquired how to live a
moral life. Confucius answered, " A workman who
wants to perfect his work first sharpens his tools. When
you are living in a country, you should serve those nobles
and ministers in that country who are men of moral
worth, and you should cultivate the friendship of the
gentlemen of that country who are men of moral
worth."

10. A disciple of Confucius enquired what institutions he would adopt for the government of an Empire.
Confucius answered, " I would use the calendar of the
Hsia dynasty ; introduce the form of carriage used
in the Yin dynasty ; and adopt the uniform of the
present dynasty. For State music I would use the
most ancient music. I would prohibit all the popular
airs in the music of the present day, and I would
banish all popular orators. The modern popular music
provokes sensuality in the people, and popular orators
are dangerous to the State."

11. Confucius remarked, " If a man takes no
thought for the morrow, he will be sorry before to-day
is out."

12. Confucius on one occasion was heard to say, "Alas! I do not now see a man who loves moral worth as he loves beauty in women."

13. Confucius, speaking of a public character of the time, remarked, "He was like one who had stolen his position. Although he knew the talents and virtues of a friend he had, yet when he came to office in the government he did nothing to bring his friend forward, and was afraid lest his friend should become his colleague."

14. Confucius remarked, "A man who expects much from himself and demands little from others will never have any enemies."

15. Confucius remarked, "A man who does not constantly say to himself 'What is the right thing to do?' I can do nothing for such a man."

16. Confucius remarked, "When a body of men sit together for a whole day without turning their conversation to some principle or truth, but only amuse themselves with small wit and smart sayings, it is a bad case."

17. Confucius remarked, "A wise and good man makes Right the substance of his being; he carries it out with judgment and good sense; he speaks it with

19

modesty ; and he attains it with sincerity :—such a man is a really good and wise man !"

18. Confucius remarked, "A wise and good man should be distressed that he has no ability ; he should never be distressed that men do not take notice of him."

19. Confucius remarked, "A wise and good man hates to die without having done anything to distinguish himself." [76]

20. Confucius remarked, "A wise man seeks for what he wants in himself; a fool seeks for it from others."

21. Confucius remarked, "A wise man is proud but not vain ; [77] he is sociable, but belongs to no party."

22. Confucius remarked, "A wise man never upholds a man because of what he says, nor does he discard what a man says because of the speaker's character."

23. A disciple of Confucius enquired : "Is there one word which may guide one in practice throughout the whole life ?" Confucius answered, "The word 'charity' [78] is perhaps the word. What you do not wish others to do unto you, do not do unto them."

[76] i.e. Of having lived in vain.
[77] Dean SWIFT says, "A really proud man is too proud to be vain."
[78] The modern fashionable word "altruism."

24. Confucius on one occasion remarked, "In my judgment of men, I do not easily award blame nor easily award praise. When I have happened to praise a man in a way which might appear beyond his deserts, you may yet be sure that I have carefully weighed my judgment. The people of to-day—there is really nothing in them to prevent one from dealing honestly with them as the men of the good old times dealt with the people of their day."

25. Confucius in his old age remarked, "In my young days, I could still obtain books which supplied information on points which the standard historical books omitted; and a man who had a horse would willingly lend it to a friend to ride. But now such times and such manners have all disappeared."

Confucius remarked, "It is plausible speech which confuses men's ideas of what is moral worth. It is petty impatience which ruins great undertakings."

27. Confucius remarked, "When a man is unpopular, it is necessary to find out why people hate him. When a man is popular, it is still necessary to find out why people like him."

28. Confucius remarked, "It is the *man* that can make his religion or the principles he professes great;

and not his religion or the principles which he professes, which can make the *man* great."

29. Confucius remarked, " To be wrong and not to reform is indeed to be wrong."

30. Confucius on one occasion remarked, "I have spent a whole day without taking food and a whole night without sleep, occupied with thinking. It was of no use. I have found it better to acquire knowledge from books."

31. Confucius remarked, "A wise and good man is occupied in the search for truth ; not in seeking for a mere living. Farming sometimes leads to starvation, and education sometimes leads to the rewards of official life. A wise man should be solicitous about truth, not anxious about poverty."

32. Confucius remarked, "There are men who attain knowledge by their understanding ; but, if they have not moral character sufficient to hold fast to it, such men will lose it again. There are men again who have attained it with their understanding and have moral character sufficient to hold fast to it; but if they do not set themselves seriously to order their knowledge aright they will not inspire respect in the people. There are lastly men who have attained it with their understanding; who have moral character

sufficient to hold fast to it; and who can set themselves
seriously to put it in order; but if they do not exercise
and make use of it in accordance with the ideals of
decency and good sense, they are not yet perfect."

33. Confucius remarked, "A wise and good man
may not show his quality in small affairs, but he can
be entrusted with great concerns. A fool may gain
distinction in small things, but he cannot be entrusted
with great concerns."

34. Confucius remarked, "Men need morality more
than the necessaries of life, such as fire and water.
I have seen men die by falling into fire or water;
but I have never seen men die from falling into
morality."

35. Confucius remarked, "When the question is
one of morality, a man need not defer to his teacher."

36. Confucius remarked, "A good, wise man is
faithful,—not merely constant."

37. Confucius remarked, "In the service of his
prince, a man should place his duty first; the matter
of pay should be with him a secondary consideration."

38. Confucius remarked, "Among really educated
men, there is no caste or race-distinction."

39. Confucius remarked, "Men of totally different
principles can never act together."

40. Confucius remarked, "Language should be intelligible and nothing more."

41. A blind music-teacher having called on Confucius, when they came to the steps of the house Confucius said to him, "Here are the steps." When they came to the mat where they were to sit, Confucius again said to him, "Here is the mat." Finally, when they had sat down, Confucius said to him, "So-and-so is here, and So-and-so is here."

Afterwards, when the blind music-teacher had left, a disciple said to Confucius, "Is that the way to behave to a music-teacher?" "Yes," replied Confucius, "that is certainly the way to behave to blind people." [79]

[79] All great musicians in ancient China were blind men.

CHAPTER XVI.

1. The head of a powerful family of nobles in Confucius' native State was preparing to commence hostilities against a small principality within that State. Two of Confucius' disciples, who were in the noble's service, came to see Confucius and informed him of it. Confucius, turning to one of these disciples, said, "Sir, is not this due to your fault? The reigning family of this principality derived its titles from ancient Emperors : besides, its land is situate within our own territory : the ruler, therefore, is a prince of the Empire. What right, then, have you to declare war against a vassal of the Emperor ?"

The disciple to whom the above was addressed, replied, "It is my lord, our Master, who wishes for this war; it is not we two, who are only his servants, that desire it."

Confucius then answered, "An ancient historian says : 'Let those who can stand the fight fall into the ranks, and let those who cannot, retire.' What is the use of a guide to a blind man if, when he is in danger, the guide does not help him and, when he falls, the guide does not lift him up? Besides, you are wrong in what you have said to excuse yourself. When a tiger or a wild animal escapes from its cage, or when a tortoise-shell or a valuable gem gets broken in its casket :—who is responsible and to blame in such a case ?"

"But now," argued one of the disciples, "this principality is very strongly fortified and is within easy reach of our most important town. If we do not reduce and take it now, it will in future be a source of anxiety and danger to the descendants of the family."

"Sir," answered Confucius, "A good man hates to make excuses when he ought to say simply 'I want it.'

"But for my part, I have been taught to believe that those who have kingdoms. and possessions should not be concerned that they have not enough possessions, but should be concerned that possessions are not equally distributed; they should not be concerned that they are poor, but should be concerned that the people are not contented. For with equal distribution there will be no poverty; with mutual good will, there will be no want; and with contentment among the people, there can be no downfall and dissolution.

"This being so, when the people outside the country do not submit, a ruler should improve the moral education at home in order to attract them; when people from outside are attracted and come to his country, the ruler should make them happy and contented.

"Now you two gentlemen," continued Confucius, "while assisting your master in his government, have done nothing to attract people from outside when they have shown signs of insubmission. At present, when the country is actually internally torn by factions, dissensions, outbreaks and dissolutions, you are doing nothing to prevent them. Instead of this, you are now going to bring on the ravages and horrors of war within our own State. I am afraid the danger in future to the stability of the house of your noble lord will not come from that small principality against which you are now going to declare war, but will arise from within the walls of your master's own palace."

2. Confucius remarked, " In the normal state of the government of an empire, the initiative and final decision in matters of religion, education, and declaration of war form the supreme prerogative of the emperor. During abnormal conditions in the government of the empire, that prerogative passes into the hands of the princes of the empire : in which case it is seldom that ten generations pass before they lose it. Should that prerogative pass into the hands of the

20

nobility of the empire, it has rarely happened that they have retained it for five generations. When subordinate officers have the power of government in their hands they generally lose their authority in the course of three generations.

"When there are order and justice in the government of a country, the supreme power of government will not be in the hands of the nobility or of a ruling class. When there are justice and order in the government of a country, the common people will not meddle with the government." [80]

3. Confucius, speaking of the state of government in his native State, remarked, "It is now five generations since the appointments to offices in the State have been taken away from the scions of the reigning houses. It is now four generations since the powers of government have passed into the hands of the ruling class of nobility. Therefore the descendants of the most ancient houses have lost all power and are now living in obscurity."

4. Confucius remarked, "There are three kinds of friendship which are beneficial and three kinds

---

[80] Confucius meant by the first what is called in Europe "an oligarchy," and by the second "democracy": both of which, according to the passage here, can never be the true normal permanent state of government in a country. The ruling class or nobility in ancient China corresponds to what Mr. RUSKIN called *squires* or country gentlemen of England.

which are injurious. Friendship with upright men, with faithful men, and with men of much information : such friendships are beneficial. Friendship with plausible men, with men of insinuating manners, and with glib-tongued men : such friendships are injurious."

5. Confucius remarked, "There are three kinds of pleasures which are beneficial and three kinds which are injurious. Pleasure derived from the study and criticism of the polite arts, pleasure in admiring and speaking of the excellent qualities of men, and pleasure in having many friends of virtue and talents : these pleasures are beneficial. Pleasure in dissipation ; in extravagance ; in mere conviviality : such pleasures are injurious."

6. Confucius remarked, "There are three kinds of errors to which men are liable when in the presence of their superiors. First, To speak out when one is not called upon to speak : that is called being froward. Secondly, To keep silence when called upon to speak : that is called being disingenuous. Thirdly, To speak out without taking into consideration the expression in the look of the person spoken to : that is called blindness."

7. Confucius remarked, "There are three things which a man should beware of in the three stages of his life. In youth, when the constitution of his body

is not yet formed, he should beware of lust. In
manhood, when his physical powers are in full vigour,
he should beware of strife. In old age, when the
physical powers are in decay, he should beware of
greed."

8. Confucius remarked, "There are three things
which a wise and good man holds in awe. He holds
in awe the Laws of God, [81] persons in authority, and
the words of wisdom of holy men. A fool, on the
other hand, does not know that there are Laws of
God; he, therefore, has no reverence for them; he is
disrespectful to persons in authority, and contemns the
words of wisdom of holy men."

9. Confucius remarked, "The highest class of men
are those who are born with a natural understanding.
The next class are those who acquire understanding by
study and application. There are others again who are
born naturally dull, but who yet by strenuous efforts,

[81] Literally, "Commandments of God." In other places we have translated
these words as Religion; for that—not the laws of Moses, Lycurgus, Christ or
Confucius, which are merely interpretations of the Laws of God,—is, we believe,
what is called Religion in Europe. The Laws of God comprise all, from the simple
law that two and two make four; that ginger is hot for the mouth; the laws that
guide the courses of sun, moon and stars, to, finally, the highest Law of Right and
Wrong in the heart of man.

"Oh that my lot might lead me in the path of holy pureness of thought and
deed, the path which august laws ordain, laws which in the highest heaven had
their birth; . . . *the power of God is mighty in them and groweth not old.*"

try to acquire understanding : such men may be considered the next class. Those who are born naturally dull and yet will not take the trouble to acquire understanding : such men are the lowest class of the people."

10. Confucius remarked, "There are nine objects which a wise man aims at. In the use of his eyes, his object is to see clearly. In the use of his ears, his object is to hear distinctly. In the expression of his look, his object is to be gracious. In his manners, his object is to be serious. In what he says, his object is to be sincere. In business, his object is to be earnest. In doubt, his object is to seek for information. In anger, his object is to think of consequences. In view of personal advantage, his object is to think of what is right."

11. Confucius remarked, "Men who, when they see what is good and honest, try to act up to it, and when they see what is bad and dishonest try to avoid it as if avoiding scalding water : such men I have known and the expressions of such principles I have heard. But men who live in retirement in order to study their aims and who practise righteousness in order to carry out their principles : the expression of such principles I have heard, but I have not seen such men."

12. Confucius, speaking of a prince lately deceased, remarked, "In his lifetime, he had a thousand teams

of horses; but on the day of his death, the people had not a good word to say of him.   On the other hand, the ancient worthies Po Yi and Shuh Ts'i, who were starved to death at the foot of a lonely mountain, are held in honour by the people to this day.   This is the meaning of the verse—

'Truly your wealth and pelf avail you nought,
To have what others want, is all you sought.' "

13. A gentleman of the Court on one occasion enquired of Confucius' son, saying : " Have you had any special lesson from your father?" "No, I have not," replied Confucius' son, "Only once when he was standing alone, and I happened to pass through the hall, he said to me : 'Have you studied poetry?' to which I replied, 'No, I have not.'   'Then,' said he, 'if you do not study poetry, you cannot make yourself agreeable in conversation.'   After that I gave myself to the study of poetry.   On another occasion when he was again standing alone, and I happened to pass through the hall, he said to me: 'Have you studied the arts,' to which I replied, 'No, I have not.'   'Then,' said he, 'if you do not study the arts, you will lack judgment and taste.'   After that, I gave myself to the study of the arts."

The gentleman of the Court, when he heard that, went away delighted, saying: "I have asked about one thing and now I have learnt about three things. In addition to what I have asked, I have learnt about the importance of the study of poetry and the arts, and also that a wise and good man does not treat even his own son with familiarity."

14. The wife of the reigning prince of a State is addressed by him as "Madame." She addresses him as "Sire." She is addressed by her people in her own State as "Madame, my lady," and her own people in speaking to people of another State, mention her as "Our good little princess." People of other States, speaking of her to her own people, call her "Madame, your princess."

CHAPTER XVII.

1. An influential officer, who was in the service of a powerful family of nobles in Confucius' native State, on one occasion expressed a wish to see Confucius, but Confucius would not go to see him. The officer then sent Confucius a present of a pig. Confucius thereupon timing his visit when the officer was not at home, called on him to tender his thanks. On returning, however, he met the officer on the way.

"Come now," said the officer to Confucius, "I want to speak to you. Now I would ask you whether he is a good man who hides the treasures of his knowledge and leaves his country to go astray?" "No," replied Confucius, "he is not." "Is he a man of understanding," asked the officer again, "who is anxious to be employed and yet misses every chance that comes to him of being employed?" "No," replied Confucius, "he is not."

"Then," said the officer, "you ought to know that days and months are passing away and time waits not for us." "Yes," replied Confucius, "I will enter the public service."

2. Confucius remarked, "Men, in their nature, are alike ; but by practice they become widely different."

3. Confucius then went on to say, "It is only men of the highest understanding and men of the grossest dullness, who do not change."

4. When Confucius on one occasion came to a small town where one of his disciples was chief Magistrate, he heard the sounds of music and singing among the people. He then, with a mischievous smile in his look, remarked, "To kill a chicken why use a knife used for slaughtering an ox ?"

"Sir," replied the disciple who was chief Magistrate of the town, "I have heard you say at one time that when the gentlemen of a country are highly educated, it makes them sympathize with the people ; and when the people are educated, it makes them easily amenable to government."

"Yes," answered Confucius, turning to his other disciples who were present, "he is right : what I said just now was only spoken in jest."

5. On one occasion a noble in Confucius' native State who held possession of an important town and was in an attitude of rebellion, invited Confucius to see him. Confucius was inclined to go. At this, Confucius' disciple, the intrepid Chung Yu, was vexed. He said,

"Indeed you cannot go! Why should you think of going to see such a man?"

"It cannot be for nothing," replied Confucius, "that he has invited me to see him. If anyone would employ me, I would establish a new empire here in the East." [82]

6. A disciple of Confucius enquired what constituted a moral life. Confucius answered, "A man who can carry out five things wherever he may be is a moral man." "What five things?" asked the disciple.

"They are," replied Confucius, "Earnestness, consideration for others, trustworthiness, diligence, and generosity. If you are earnest, you will never meet with want of respect. If you are considerate to others, you will win the hearts of the people. If you are trustworthy, men will trust you. If you are diligent, you will be successful in your undertakings. If you are generous, you will find plenty of men who are willing to serve you."

7. On one occasion a noble of a certain State having rebelled against the legitimate authority, invited Confucius to see him. Confucius was inclined to go, but Confucius' disciple, the intrepid Chung Yu, said to

[82] *i.e,* Of China. The Imperial domain then was in the Western part of China.

Confucius: "Sir, I have heard you say at one time that a wise and good man will not associate even with those persons who are nearly related to him, when such persons have been found guilty of evil-doing. Now this man is holding a town in actual rebellion against authority? How is it that you can think of going to see him?"

"Yes," replied Confucius, "I have said that. But is it not also said that if a thing is really hard you may pound it and yet it will not crack; if a thing is really white, you may smirch it, and yet it will not become black. And am I, after all, only a bitter gourd to be hung up and not eaten at all?"

8. Confucius once remarked to a disciple, saying: "Have you ever heard of the six virtues and their failures?" "No," replied the disciple. "Sit down then," said Confucius, "and I will tell you.

"First there is the mere love of morality: that alone, without culture, degenerates into fatuity. Secondly, there is the mere love of knowledge: that alone, without culture, tends to dilettantism. Thirdly, there is the mere love of honesty: that alone, without culture, produces heartlessness. Fourthly, there is the mere love of uprightness: that alone, without culture, leads to tyranny."[63] Fifthly, there is the mere love of courage: that alone, without culture, produces recklessness. Sixthly, there is the mere love of strength of character: that alone, without culture, produces eccentricity."

9. Confucius on one occasion remarked to his disciples, "My young friends, why do you not study poetry? Poetry calls out the sentiment. It stimulates observation. It enlarges the sympathies and moderates the resentment felt against injustice. Poetry, in fact, while it has lessons for the duties of social life, at the same time makes us acquainted with the animate and inanimate objects in nature."[64]

10. Confucius once said to his son, "You should give yourself to the study of the first two books in the Book of Ballads, Songs and Psalms. A man who has not studied those books will be out of his element wherever he goes."

11. Confucius was once heard to say, "Men speak about Art! Art! Do you really think that merely

[63] "The most cruel and unmerciful of men, perhaps, is an honest bureaucrat; and the most tyrannical, an upright priest, especially of Protestant dissenting Christianity, or, as now the species of upright priests is extinct—a disciple of Herbert Spencer."—A modern Rochefoucauld.

[64] WORDSWORTH says of poetry that it tends to —
"Nourish the imagination in her growth,
"And give the mind that apprehensive power
"Whereby she is made quick to recognise
"The moral properties and scope of things."

means painting and sculpture? Men speak about music! Music! Do you think that means merely bells, drums, and musical instruments?"

12. Confucius remarked, "A man who is austere in his look, but a weakling and a coward at heart—is he not like one of your small, mean people : yea, is he not like a sneaking thief or a cowardly pickpocket ?"

13. Confucius remarked, "Your meek men of respectability in a place, are they who unmercifully destroy all sense of moral sentiment in man."

14. Confucius remarked, "To preach in the public streets the commonplaces which you have picked up on the way is to throw away all your finer feelings."

15. Confucius, speaking of the public men of his time, remarked : "These despicable men! How is it possible to serve the interests of the country in company with such men ? Before they gain their position, their only anxiety is how to obtain it ; and after they have obtained the position, their sole anxiety is lest they should lose it. In their anxiety lest they should lose their position, there is nothing which they would not do."

16. Confucius remarked, "In old times men had three kinds of imperfections in their characters, which perhaps now are not to be found. Passionate, impetuous

men in old times loved independence ; but passionate impetuosity nowadays shows itself in wild licence. Proud men in old times were modest and reserved, but pride nowadays shows itself in touchiness and vulgar bad-temper. Simple men in old times were artless and straightforward, but simplicity nowadays hides cunning."

17. Confucius remarked, "With plausible speech and fine manners will seldom be found moral character."

18. Confucius remarked, "I hate the way in which scarlet dims the perception for vermilion. I hate the way in which the modern popular airs are liable to spoil the taste for good music. Finally, I hate the way in which smartness of speech in men is liable to destroy kingdoms and ruin families."

19. Confucius was once heard to say, "I would rather not speak at all."

"But if you do not speak, sir," asked a disciple, "What shall we, your disciples, learn from you to be taught to others?"

"Look at the Heaven there," answered Confucius, "Does it speak? And yet the seasons run their appointed courses and all things in nature grow up in their time. Look at the Heaven there : does it speak ? "

20. A man who wanted to see Confucius called on him. Confucius, not wishing to see him, sent to say he was sick. When the servant with the message went to the door, Confucius took up his musical instrument and sang aloud purposely to let the visitor hear it and know that he was not really sick.

21. A disciple of Confucius enquired about the period of three years' mourning for parents, remarking that one year was long enough.

"For," said he, "if a gentleman neglects the Arts and usages of life for three years, he will lose his knowledge of them ; and if he put aside music for three years, he will entirely forget it. Again, even in the ordinary course of nature, in one year the old corn is mown away to give place to new corn which springs up, and in one year we burn through all the different kinds of wood produced in all the seasons. I believe, therefore, that after the completion of one year, mourning may cease."

Confucius answered, " If, after one year's mourning, you were to eat good food and wear fine clothes, would you feel at ease ? "

"I should," replied the disciple. "Then," answered Confucius, "if you can feel at ease, do it. But a good man during the whole period of three years' mourning, does not enjoy good food when he eats it, and derives no pleasure from music when he hears it; when he is lodged in comfort, he does not feel at ease : therefore, he does not do anything of those things. You, however, since you feel at ease, can, of course, do them."

Afterwards, when the disciple had left, Confucius remarked, "What a man without moral feeling he is? It is only three years after his birth that a child is able to leave the arms of his parents. Now the period of three years' mourning for parents is universally observed throughout the Empire. As to that man,—I wonder if he was one who did not enjoy the affection of his parents when he was a child!"

22. Confucius remarked, "It is really a bad case when a man simply eats his full meals without applying his mind to anything at all during the whole day. Are there not such things as gambling and games of skill? To do one of those things even is better than to do nothing at all."

23. A disciple of Confucius, the intrepid Chung Yu, enquired : "Is not valour a quality important to a gentleman?"

"A gentleman," answered Confucius, "esteems what is right as of the highest importance. A gentleman who has valour, but is without a knowledge and love of what is right, is likely to commit a crime. A man of the people who has courage, but is without the knowledge and love of what is right, is likely to become a robber."

24. A disciple of Confucius enquired, "Has a wise and good man also his hatreds?"

"Yes," answered Confucius, "he has his hatreds. He hates those who love to expatiate on the evil doings of others. He hates those who, themselves living low, disreputable lives, try to detract those who are trying to live a higher life. He hates those who are valourous, but without judgment and manners. He hates those who are energetic and bold, but narrow-minded and selfish."

"And you," continued Confucius, addressing the disciple, "have you also your hatreds?"

"Yes," replied the disciple, "I hate those who are censorious and believe themselves to be clever. I hate those who are presumptuous and believe themselves to be brave. I hate those who ransack out the secret misdoings of others in order to proclaim them, and believe themselves to be upright."

22

25. Confucius remarked, "Of all people in the world, young women and servants are the most difficult to keep in the house. If you are familiar with them, they forget their position. But if you keep them at a distance, they are discontented."

26. Confucius remarked, "If a man after forty is an object of dislike to men, he will continue to be so to the end of his days."

CHAPTER XVIII.

1. At the time of the downfall of the Imperial Yin dynasty (the one preceding that under which Confucius lived) of the three members of the Imperial family, one left the country;[86] one became a court jester; and one, who spoke the truth to the Emperor, was put to death.

Confucius, remarking on the above, said, "The House of Yin in their last days had three men of moral character."

2. Confucius remarked of a well-known worthy of the time : "As Minister of Justice, he was three times dismissed from office. People then said to him, 'Is it not time for you to leave the country?' But he answered, 'If I honestly do my duty, where shall I go to serve men without being liable to be dismissed in the same way? If I am willing to sacrifice my sense of duty, it is not necessary for me to leave my native country to find employment.'"

3. The reigning prince of a certain State on one occasion wished to employ Confucius, remarking, how-

---

[86] He was a remote ancestor of Confucius,

ever, "I cannot make him a Minister of State, but I will make him a privy Councillor."

The prince further remarked, "I am old now. I shall not be able to use his advice."

When Confucius heard what the prince said, he immediately took his departure from the country.

4. The Prime Minister who held the power of government in Confucius' native State, after Confucius had risen to be Minister of State (Minister of Justice), having on one occasion received a troupe of actresses from another State was so occupied with them that there was no meeting of ministers at the Palace for three days. Confucius thereupon resigned, and left his own country.

5. When Confucius was on his travels, an eccentric person once passing by him, sang aloud—

> "O Phœnix bird ! O Phœnix bird,
> "Where is the glory of your prime ?
> "The past,—'t is useless now to change,
> "Care for the future yet is time.
> "Renounce! give up your chase in vain ;
> "For those who serve in Court and State
> "Dire peril follows in their train."

Confucius then alighted and wished to speak with him ; but the eccentric man hastened away so that Confucius had no chance of speaking with him.

6. On another occasion, Confucius on his travels saw two men working in the fields. He sent a disciple, the intrepid Chung Yu, to enquire for the ford.

When Chung Yu came up to the men, one of them said to him : " Who is he that is holding the reins in the carriage there ?" Chung Yu answered, " It is Confucius." " Is it not Confucius of Lu," asked the man. " Yes," replied Chung Yu. " Then," rejoined the other, "he knows the ford."

Chung Yu then turned to the other of the two men, who said to him : "Who are you, sir?" "I am Chung Yu," replied Confucius' disciple. "Are you not a disciple of Confucius ? " asked the man. "Yes," replied Chung Yu. Then the man said : " All men in the world are now in a hopeless drift : who can do any-thing to change it ? Nevertheless, it is better to follow those who renounce the world altogether than to run after those who only run from one prince to another." After saying that, the man went on with his work on the field without stopping again to take any notice of Chung Yu's question.

When Chung Yu returned and reported what the man said, Confucius heaved a heavy sigh, and said, " I cannot live with the beasts of the field and birds of the air. If I do not live and associate with mankind, with whom shall I go to live? Besides, if the world was in order, there would then be no need for one to do anything to change it."

7. On another occasion when Confucius was on his travels, a disciple, the intrepid Chung Yu, got separated from the party. Chung Yu met an old man carrying across his shoulders, on a staff, a basket for weeds. Chung Yu said to him, "Have you seen the Teacher sir?" The old man looked at him and replied gruffly, "Your body has never known toil and you cannot tell the difference between the five kinds of grain : who is your Teacher?" With that, the old man planted his staff on the ground and fell to his work, weeding the ground. Chung Yu, however, laid his hands across his breast and respectfully waited.

Afterwards, the old man took Chung Yu to his home and made him pass a night in his house, killing a fowl and making millet pudding for him to eat. The old man also presented his two sons to Chung Yu.

The next day Chung Yu went on his way and, on rejoining Confucius, reported his adventure. "He is a hermit," said Confucius, and sent Chung Yu back to see him; but when Chung Yu got to the place the old man was nowhere to be found.

When Chung Yu again returned, Confucius said, "It is not right to refuse to enter the public service. For if it is wrong to ignore the duties arising out of the relations between the members of a family, how is it right to ignore the duties a man owes to his sovereign and country. A man who withdraws himself from the world for no other reason than to show his personal purity of motive, is one who breaks up one of the greatest ties in the foundation of society. A good and wise man, on the other hand, who enters the public service, tries to carry out what he thinks to be right. As to the failure of right principles to make progress, he is well aware of that."

8. Confucius, speaking of six worthies, famous in ancient times as men who withdrew themselves from the world, remarked of two of them, Po Yi and Shuh-ts'i, that they withdrew from the world because they would not give up their high aims, and, in that way, had not to put up with dishonour to their persons; of two others who finally also withdrew from the world, Confucius remarked that they gave up high aims and put up with dishonour to their persons, but in whatever they said were found reasonable and, in whatever they did, were found commendable; finally, of the last two of the six worthies, Confucius remarked that they lived

strictly as recluses and refused altogether to hold communication with the world, but they were pure in their lives and so, entirely secluding themselves from the world, they rightly used their discretion.

"As for myself," said Confucius, finally, "I act differently from those men I have mentioned above, I have no course for which I am predetermined, and no course against which I am predetermined."

9. [This section merely gives the names of the famous musicians and great artists of the time who, falling on a time of decay of art and failure of art patronage, had to wander scattered about from one State to another; one, it is said, went out over sea,—perhaps to Japan!]

10. The original Founder of the reigning house of Confucius' native State, who was known as our Lord of Chou, in his advice to his son and successor said : "A ruler should never neglect his near relations. He should never give his great ministers cause to complain that their advice is not taken. Without some great reason, he should never discard his old connections. He should never expect from a man that he will be able to do everything."

11. [This section merely gives the names of eight famous gentlemen of the time.]

CHAPTER XIX.

1. A disciple of Confucius remarked, "A gentleman in presence of danger should be ready to give up his life ; in view of personal advantage, he should think of what is right; in worship, he should be devout and serious; in mourning, he should show heartfelt grief: the above is about the sum of the duties of a gentleman."

2. The same disciple remarked, "If a man holds fast to godliness without enlarging his mind ; if a man believes in truth, but is not steadfast in holding to his principles— such a man may as well leave such things alone."

3. The same disciple was on one occasion asked about friendship by the pupils of one of his fellow disciples. He answered by asking the pupils, "What did your teacher say on the subject?" "Our teacher," replied the pupils, "said, 'Those whom you find good, make friends with ; those whom you find not good, turn your back upon.'"

"That," replied Confucius' disciple who was asked, "is different from what I have been taught. A wise and good man honours worthy men and is tolerant to all men. He knows how to commend those

23

who excel in anything and make allowance for those
who are ignorant. Now, if we ourselves are really
worthy, we should be tolerant to all men; but if
we ourselves are not worthy, men will turn their
backs upon us. How can we turn our backs upon
them?"

4. A disciple of Confucius remarked, "Even in
any small and unimportant branch of an art or
accomplishment, there is always something worthy of
consideration; but if the attention to it is pushed too
far, it is liable to degenerate into a hobby; for that
reason a wise man never occupies himself with it."

5. The same disciple of Confucius remarked, "A
man who from day to day knows exactly what he
has yet to learn, and from month to month does not
forget what he has learnt, will surely become a man of
culture."

6. The same disciple remarked, "If you study
extensively and are steadfast in your aim, investigate
carefully what you learn and apply it to your own
personal conduct; in that way, you cannot fail in
attaining a moral life."

7. The same disciple remarked, "As workmen
work in their workshops to learn their trade, so a
scholar gives himself to study in order to get wisdom."

8. The same disciple remarked, "A fool always has an excuse ready when he does wrong."

9. The same disciple remarked, "A good and wise man appears different from three points of view. When you look at him from a distance he appears severe ; when you approach him he is gracious ; when you hear him speak, he is serious."

10. The same disciple remarked, "A wise man, as a ruler, first obtains the confidence of the people before he puts them to hard work—which otherwise would be regarded by the people as oppression. A wise man, as a public servant, first obtains the confidence of those whom he serves before he ventures to point out their errors ; otherwise his superiors will only regard what he says as prompted by a desire to · find fault."

11. The same disciple remarked, "When a man can keep himself strictly within bounds where the major points of the principles of morality are concerned, he may be allowed to use his discretion in the minor points."

12. A disciple of Confucius, speaking of the pupils of another disciple, remarked, "Those young gentlemen are well enough in matters of manners and deportment, which are mere minor matters ; but as

regards the foundation of a true education, they are as yet nowhere."

When the disciple whose pupils were thus animadverted upon, heard the remark, he said to the other disciple : "There you are wrong. In teaching men, what are the things which a good and wise man should consider it of first importance that he should teach ; and what are the things which he should consider of secondary importance, and which he may allow himself to neglect ? As in dealing with plants, so one must deal with pupils and class them according to their capabilities. A good and wise man in teaching, should not befool his students. For it is only the most holy men who can at once grasp the beginning and end of principles."

13. A disciple of Confucius remarked, " An officer who has exceptional abilities, more than sufficient to carry out his duties, should devote himself to study. A student who has exceptional abilities, more than sufficient to carry on his studies, should enter the public service."

14. A disciple of Confucius remarked, " In mourning, the only thing indispensable is heart-felt grief."

15. The same disciple, speaking of another disciple, remarked, " My friend can do things which nobody

else can do, but he is not quite perfect in his moral character."

16. Another disciple of Confucius, speaking of the same disciple alluded to above, remarked, "What a style that man carries about with him ! It is really difficult to live out a moral life along with such a man !"

17. The same disciple remarked, "I have heard the Master say, 'Men often do not themselves know what is really in them until they have to mourn the death of their parents.'"

18. The same disciple remarked, "I have heard the Master, speaking of the filial piety of a nobleman, say, "What other things he did on the occasion of the death of his father, other men can do. But what he did in keeping the old servants of his father, and in following out the policy of his father, men will find it difficult to do."

19. The Prime Minister in Confucius' native State having on one occasion appointed an officer to be Chief Criminal Judge, the officer came to a disciple of Confucius for advice. The disciple then said to the officer : " Rulers have long failed in their duties, and the people have long lived in a state of disorganisation. If you should discover enough evidence to convict a man,

feel pity and be merciful to him ; do not feel glad at your discovery." [86]

20. A disciple of Confucius, speaking of an infamous emperor and tyrant of ancient times, remarked: " His wickedness was, after all, not so bad as tradition reports. Therefore a wise man will not persist in a low, disreputable life in defiance of what men may say : for otherwise, people will give him credit for all the wickednesses that are in the world."

21. The same disciple remarked, " The failings of a great man are eclipses of the sun and moon. When he fails, all men see it ; but, when he recovers from his failing, all men look up to him as before."

22. An officer of the Court in a certain State asked a disciple of Confucius, "From whom did Confucius learn the principles he taught ?"

[86] Welchen Weg musste nicht die Menschheit machen bis sie dahin gelangte, auch gegen Schuldige gelind, gegen Verbrecher schonend, gegen auch Unmenschlich menschlich, zu sein. Gewiss waren es Männer gottlicher Natur, die diess zuerst lehrten, die ihr Leben damit zu brachten, die Aüsübung mochlich zu machen, und zu beschleunigen. (What a long way mankind must travel before they arrive at the stage when they know how to be tender to evil-doers, considerate to law-breakers, and human even to the inhuman. Truly they were men of divine nature who first taught this and who gave up their lives in order to make the realisation of this possible and to hasten the practice of it.)—GOETHE, *Wilhelm Meister*.

People now speak of " Progress." Progress, according to GOETHE, here would seem to mean that mankind should "progress" towards being more and more *human*. Judged by this, China, two thousand years ago, seemed to have already made real progress in civilisation.

The disciple answered, "The principles of religion and morality held by the ancients have not all disappeared. Even now among men, those who are wise and worthy understand the great principles of the system, and those who are not wise, and even unworthy men, understand the lesser principles. As to our Teacher, he had no need to learn ; and even if he had to learn, why should he necessarily have had one special teacher?"

23. An officer of the Court in Confucius' native State, expressing admiration for a disciple of Confucius, remarked in presence of the other Court officers : " In my opinion this disciple of Confucius is superior to Confucius himself."

Afterwards, when somebody reported what the officer had said to the disciple above referred to, the latter said: " Let me use the comparison of two buildings. The wall of my building only reaches to the shoulders ; one has only to look over and he can see all that is valuable in the apartments. But the wall of the Master's building is hundreds of feet high. If one does not find the door to enter by, he can never see the treasures of art and the glory of the men that are in the holy temple. Perhaps, however, there are few men who have found the door. I do not therefore wonder that the officer spoke as he did."

24. The same Court officer was once heard to abuse the character of Confucius. The same disciple on hearing of it, said: "It is no use for him to do that. Confucius can never be abused. The moral and intellectual endowments of other men as compared with those of Confucius are as hillocks and mounds which you may climb over. But Confucius is like the sun and moon. You can never jump over them. You may break your neck in trying to do it, but the sun and moon will remain as they are. In trying to do that, you only show your want of sense in not knowing what you can do."

25. Another man on another occasion said to the same disciple, "But you are too earnest and conscientious. How can Confucius be superior to you?"

"For one word," replied the disciple, "an educated man is held to be a man of understanding, and for one word he is held to be foolish. You should therefore be careful indeed in what you say. Now Confucius cannot be equalled, just as no man can climb up to the sky. If Confucius, our Master, had been born' an emperor or a prince, he would then have done those things told of the holy kings of old: 'What he lays down becomes law: what he orders is carried out;

whither he beckons, the people follow; wherever his influence is felt, there is peace; while he lives, he lives honoured by the whole world; when he dies he is mourned for by the whole world.' How is it possible for a man to equal Confucius, our Master!"

CHAPTER XX.

1. The ancient Emperor Yao, when in his old age
he abdicated the throne in favour of his successor,
Shun, thus gave him charge: "Hail to thee, O Shun!
The God-ordained order of succession now rests upon
thy person. Hold fast with thy heart and soul to the
true middle course of right. If there shall be distress
and want among the people within the Empire, the title
and honour which God has given to thee will be taken
away from thee for ever."

Afterwards the Emperor Shun, when he abdicated
in favour of his successor, the great Yü, used the same
language in giving him charge.

The Emperor T'ang, when he ascended the Imperial
throne, thus offered up his prayer to God : "I, Li, who
am one of thy children, do here take upon me to offer
up to thee in sacrifice this black heifer, and to announce
to Thee, O supreme and sovereign God, that sinners
I shall not dare to pardon; and, in the choice of Thy
servants, I pray Thee, O God, that thou wilt let me
know Thy will and pleasure. If I do sin against Thee,
let not the people suffer for my sin. But if the people

shall sin against Thee, let me alone bear the penalty of their iniquities."

With the inauguration of the Chou dynasty, the country was greatly prosperous ; but only the good were rich.

The Emperors guided themselves by the principle contained in these words: "Although there are men attached and related to our person, yet we do not consider them equal in value to men of moral character. If the people fail in their conduct, it is we alone who are to blame."

The Emperors set themselves to adjust and enforce uniformity in the use of weights and measures; to organise the administration and laws ; to re-establish disused offices : in this way the administration throughout the Empire was well carried out. They restored extinct families of nobles ; called to office retired men of virtue and learning : thus the people throughout the Empire gladly acknowledged their authority. What they paid serious attention to were food for the people, rituals and mourning for the dead, and religious services. By considerateness, they won the heart of the people ; by good faith, they caused the people to have confidence in them ; by diligence in business, what they undertook prospered; by their fair and impartial dealing, the people were contented.

2. A disciple of Confucius enquired of him, "What should be done in order to conduct the government of a country?"

Confucius answered, "In the conduct of government there are five good principles to be kept in mind and respected, and there are four bad principles to be avoided."

"What are the five good principles to be respected?" asked the disciple.

Confucius replied, "First, to benefit the people without wasting the resources of the country; Secondly, to encourage labour without giving cause for complaint; Thirdly, to desire for the enjoyments of life without being covetous; Fourthly, to be dignified without being supercilious; Fifthly, to inspire awe without being severe."

"But," again asked the disciple, "What do you mean by 'To benefit the people without wasting the resources of the country'?"

"It is," replied Confucius, "to encourage the people to undertake such profitable labour as will best benefit them, without its being necessary to give them any assistance out of the public revenue; that is what is meant by, 'To benefit the people without wasting the resources of the country.'"

Confucius then went on to say, "In the employment of the people in forced labour on works for the public good, if you select those who are most able to bear it, who will have any cause for complaint? Make it your aim to wish for moral well-being and you will never be liable to be covetous. A wise and good man, whether dealing with a few people or with many, with great matters or with small, is never presumptuous and never regards anything as beneath his notice or as unworthy of serious and careful attention : that is what is meant by being dignified without being supercilious. And, finally, to inspire awe without being severe, a wise and good man has only to watch over every minute detail connected with his daily life, not only of conduct and bearing, but even in minor details of dress, so as to produce an effect upon the public mind, which, without these influences, could only have been produced by fear."

"Now I understand," said the disciple, "But what do you mean by the four bad principles of which you have spoken?"

"First," replied Confucius, "is cruelty; that is, the undue punishment of crimes committed through

ignorance arising out of a neglected education. Secondly,
tyranny of that kind which renders people liable to
punishment for offences without first clearly giving public
notice. Thirdly, heartlessness ; which means to leave
orders in abeyance and uncertainty, and suddenly to
enforce their performance by punishment. And lastly,
meanness ; to treat your subordinates as if bartering
with them exactly and meanly : that is called behaving
like professional men and not like gentlemen."

3. Confucius remarked, " Without religion a man
cannot be a good and wise man ; without knowledge of
the arts and of the principles of art, a man cannot form his
judgment ; without the knowledge of the use of language,
a man cannot judge of and know the character of men."

[This last chapter sums up the teaching of
Confucius : the 1st section shows the grand and high
principle of responsibility in the rulers towards God
as the foundation of government, and gives also the
important functions necessary for the carrying out of
good government ; the 2nd section gives what principles
a ruler must constantly guide himself by and what
principles he must avoid ; the last section sums up the
three things necessary for the education and formation
of the character of a gentleman : three things, namely,
Religion, a knowledge of the Arts, and Literature.]

www.ingramcontent.com/pod-product-compliance
Lightning Source LLC
Chambersburg PA
CBHW030837270326
41928CB00007B/1089